BestMasters

Mit **„BestMasters“** zeichnet Springer die besten Masterarbeiten aus, die an renommierten Hochschulen in Deutschland, Österreich und der Schweiz entstanden sind. Die mit Höchstnote ausgezeichneten Arbeiten wurden durch Gutachter zur Veröffentlichung empfohlen und behandeln aktuelle Themen aus unterschiedlichen Fachgebieten der Naturwissenschaften, Psychologie, Technik und Wirtschaftswissenschaften. Die Reihe wendet sich an Praktiker und Wissenschaftler gleichermaßen und soll insbesondere auch Nachwuchswissenschaftlern Orientierung geben.

Springer awards **“BestMasters”** to the best master’s theses which have been completed at renowned Universities in Germany, Austria, and Switzerland. The studies received highest marks and were recommended for publication by supervisors. They address current issues from various fields of research in natural sciences, psychology, technology, and economics. The series addresses practitioners as well as scientists and, in particular, offers guidance for early stage researchers.

Daniel Dorrer

Introduction of IReF

The Development of an Integrated System for Achieving Harmonised Supervisory Reporting in the European Union

Springer Gabler

Daniel Dorrer
Quantitatives Asset and Risk
Management
Fachhochschule des BFI Wien
Vienna, Austria

ISSN 2625-3577 ISSN 2625-3615 (electronic)
BestMasters
ISBN 978-3-658-46446-2 ISBN 978-3-658-46447-9 (eBook)
https://doi.org/10.1007/978-3-658-46447-9

This Springer Gabler imprint is published by the registered company Springer Fachmedien Wiesbaden GmbH, part of Springer Nature.
The registered company address is: Abraham-Lincoln-Str. 46, 65189 Wiesbaden, Germany

Abstract

This master's thesis aims to provide a comprehensive understanding of the regulatory framework and technical aspects of integrated supervisory reporting within the Eurozone. It addresses the practical need for transparency and consistency in reporting standards amidst evolving financial landscapes. Key research questions focus on the impact of integrated supervisory reporting on risk management practices, regulatory compliance and overall financial stability.

This paper employs a multi-faceted research approach to examine the impact of integrated supervisory reporting within the Eurozone. A comprehensive literature review forms the foundation, drawing insights from academic papers, reports and regulatory documents. To enhance the reader's understanding, case studies as practical illustrations will be incorporated. In addition, expert interviews with professionals directly involved in the development and implementation of reporting standards at the European Central Bank and National Central Banks enrich the research with practical perspectives.

The findings of this thesis underscore the significant benefits of integrated supervisory reporting on various aspects of the financial landscape within the Eurozone. Through the analysis of integrated reporting frameworks, it becomes evident that these initiatives have significantly simplified reporting processes while improving data quality and streamlining reporting processes. Furthermore, the integration of national reporting systems, highlights the importance of aligning national practices with European-wide standards.

Contents

Abbreviations

BDD	Banking Data Dictionary
BIRD	Banks' Integrated Reporting Dictionary
BIS	Bank for International Settlements
BRRD	Bank Recovery and Resolution Directive
BSI	Balance Sheet Items
BTS	Binding Technical Standards
COREP	Common Reporting
CRD	Capital Requirements Directive
CRR	Capital Requirements Regulation
DBMS	Database Management System
DGSD	Deposit Guarantee Schemes Directive
DPM	Data Point Model
EBA	European Banking Authority
ECB	European Central Bank
EDIS	European Deposit Insurance Scheme
EEC	European Economic Community
EIL	Enriched Input Layer
EIOPA	European Insurance and Occupational Pensions Authority
ELDM	Enriched Logical Data Model
EMU	Economic and Monetary Union
ERD	Entity-Relationship Diagram
ERF	European Regulatory Framework
ERM	Entity-Relationship Model
ESCB	European System of Central Banks

ESFS	European System of Financial Supervisors
ESMA	European Securities and Markets Authority
ESRB	European Systemic Risk Board
EU	European Union
FINREP	Financial Reporting
FSAP	Financial Services Action Plan
FV	Fair Value
GRISS	Groupe de Réflexion on the Integration of Statistical and Supervisory Data
IFRS	International Financial Reporting Standards
IL	Input Layer
IMF	International Monetary Fund
IReF	Integrated Reporting Framework
ITS	Implementation Technical Standards
LDM	Logical Data Models
MFI	Monetary and Financial Institutions
MiFID	Markets in Financial Instruments Directive
MIR	MFI Interest Rate Statistics
NCA	National Competent Authorities
NCB	National Central Bank
NROL	Non-Reference Output Layer
OeNB	Oesterreichische Nationalbank
PDM	Physical Data Models
RM	Relational Model
ROL	Reference Output Layer
RTS	Regulatory Technical Standards
SDD	Single Data Dictionary
SDMX	Statistical Data and Metadata eXchange
SHS-S	Securities Holdings Statistics
SQL	Structured Query Language
SRB	Single Rulebook
SRM	Single Resolution Mechanism
SSM	Single Supervisory Mechanism
TEU	Treaty on European Union
TFEU	Treaty on the Functioning of the European Union
US-GAAP	United States Generally Accepted Accounting Principles
VTL	Validation and Transformation Language
XBRL	eXtensible Business Reporting Language
XII	XBRL International Inc
XML	Extensible Markup Language

List of Figures

1 Introduction

1.1 Topic and Relevance

In today's increasingly interconnected world, the dynamics of the global financial landscape have undergone a profound transformation. Financial markets have expanded their reach across borders, companies are operating on a global scale and private households are also increasingly participating in international transactions.[1] Against this backdrop, an urgent problem arises in the form of a multitude of regulations that span the globe, making the financial world one of the most complicated and diverse regulatory landscapes. Divergent financial regulations across countries can create inefficiencies and increase compliance costs for businesses and individuals participating in these markets. The harmonisation of financial regulations facilitates smoother cross-border transactions and investments, reducing friction within the global economy. Harmonised rules may enhance investor confidence by providing a consistent regulatory environment. As investors gain confidence in the stability and transparency of financial markets, they are more likely to participate and invest, potentially boosting economic growth.[2] Consequently, harmonisation of reporting standards in the banking industry and its impact on risk management, regulatory compliance and financial stability is an area of considerable scientific interest. Conducting research to identify ways to harmonise rules can lead to more efficient financial markets, benefiting both businesses and consumers.[3]

---

[1] Beck (2024) pp. 1–3.

[2] Challapalli (2023) p. 55.

[3] Hahn (2010) pp. 94–97.

D. Dorrer, *Introduction of IReF*, BestMasters,
https://doi.org/10.1007/978-3-658-46447-9_1

Through an examination of standardized reporting frameworks in the banking sector, this research paper provides an opportunity to assess the effectiveness of standardized reporting frameworks in improving financial transparency, comparability and accountability across institutions. The results of this research can contribute to the existing literature on accounting standards, regulatory practices and risk management strategies. Additionally, they can offer insight into the potential benefits and challenges associated with implementing such frameworks at both regional and national levels, thus informing future research in financial regulation and governance.

The introduction of the Integrated Reporting Framework (IReF) system and the Banks' Integrated Reporting Dictionary (BIRD) by the European Central Bank (ECB) signifies a push towards greater harmonisation and standardization of reporting practices. Understanding the impact of these initiatives, such as the IReF system and BIRD, on risk management practices, regulatory compliance and overall financial stability is crucial for financial institutions as they navigate the evolving regulatory landscape. The research outcomes of this study can provide valuable insights to policymakers, central banks and financial institutions in assessing the effectiveness and implications of adopting reporting standards. These results potentially help these institutions optimize their risk management, streamline compliance procedures and ultimately contribute to the overall stability of the financial system in the euro area.

1.2 Research Question

Against the backdrop of the divergent and ever-changing financial landscape, this master's thesis emphasises the topic of financial markets regulation to answer the following research question:

> *"What impact does the harmonisation of reporting standards at the European Central Bank, through the introduction of the Integrated Reporting Framework (IReF) system and the establishment of the Banks' Integrated Reporting Dictionary (BIRD), have on risk management practices, regulatory compliance and overall financial stability among various financial institutions operating in the Eurozone?"*

To answer the research question, the following hypotheses are tested:

- The implementation of the Integrated Reporting Framework system and the Banks' Integrated Reporting Dictionary by the European Central Bank leads to improved risk management practices among financial institutions operating in the Eurozone.

- Adoption of the Integrated Reporting Framework system and the Banks' Integrated Reporting Dictionary enhances regulatory compliance among financial institutions operating in the Eurozone.
- The harmonization of reporting standards through the Integrated Reporting Framework system and the Banks' Integrated Reporting Dictionary positively influences overall financial stability within the Eurozone's financial markets.

1.3 Methodological Approach

The first part of this master's thesis will focus on a comprehensive literature review. This method entails reviewing existing literature, including academic papers, books and reports, to gather information, theories and empirical findings related to the research topic. The primary aim of this research is to establish a foundational knowledge base concerning reporting standards and frameworks. The author will specifically examine the evolution of existing reporting standards within the European Central Bank (ECB) and the Austrian Central Bank (OeNB). This foundational knowledge will provide context for the subsequent chapters that delve into the Banks' Integrated Reporting Dictionary (BIRD) and Integrated Reporting Framework (IReF). To provide a broader context, the paper will commence by discussing the history of regulatory reporting. Following that, current reporting practices, each of which plays a significant role in shaping contemporary reporting practices, will be examined. Since the OeNB has one of the leading roles in the development of supervisory reporting within the ECB due to the invention of the Basic Cube, the master's thesis intends to investigate whether the existing system can be integrated into the IReF system. Through an examination of these current practices, the reader gains insights into the existing reporting landscape.

Having laid the theoretical foundation, the second section of this master's thesis will provide a comprehensive exposition of the technical aspects of the integrated reporting framework. This section will examine into the intricate details of the framework, exploring its underlying technical components and mechanisms. To enhance the reader's understanding, real-life case studies as practical illustrations will be incorporated. These case studies will exemplify the application of the integrated reporting framework in real-world scenarios, offering valuable insights into its practical implementation and effectiveness for risk management practices, regulatory compliance and overall financial stability among various financial institutions operating in the Eurozone. The final part of this master's thesis will address the characteristics of the Integrated Reporting Framework and examine the significance of the Banks' Integrated Reporting Dictionary. Here, the key features and principles of the IReF, as well as the role played by the BIRD in facilitating integrated reporting practices, will be explained. Furthermore, an analysis of the implementation process addressing its challenges will be conducted.

Expert interviews will play a fundamental role in improving the depth of this master's thesis and will enable the integration of real-life insights and practical expertise into the research findings. By interviewing experts who are directly involved in the development and implementation of reporting standards at the European Central Bank and the Austrian National Bank, the thesis will be enriched with first-hand perspectives.

Literature Review 2

2.1 Overview of the Regulatory Framework in the Eurozone

In the Eurozone, a complex and robust regulatory framework plays a crucial role in maintaining financial stability. This framework is designed to address the challenges by the different economies and financial institutions within the Eurozone while also encouraging economic growth and ensuring the integrity of the financial markets. In addition to the fundamental goals of stability and growth, a key objective of the Eurozone's regulatory framework is the harmonisation of financial markets, achieved through regulatory reporting practices. The concept of harmonising regulatory reporting rules emerged with the introduction of Basel I in 1988 and has since undergone further development in the dynamic landscape of the financial market.[1]

Since the financial crisis, new reporting requirements have proven crucial for supervisory, resolution and statistical purposes. These requirements provide authorities at both EU and national level with important information to fulfil their tasks, contributing to overarching objectives such as financial stability, market integrity and consumer and investor protection in Eurozone. These statistical, prudential and resolution reporting requirements facilitate the conduct of monetary policy and enable macroprudential oversight of the financial system, while ensuring the resolvability of institutions when necessary.[2] The current regulatory reporting landscape in the Eurozone consists of various actors, including reporting entities and authorities and is based on cooperation between them. These

[1] Shavshukov/Zhuravleva (2023) pp. 1–2.

[2] Benczur et al. (2017) pp. 1–3.

D. Dorrer, *Introduction of IReF*, BestMasters,
https://doi.org/10.1007/978-3-658-46447-9_2

frameworks consist of a variety of national, European and international requirements. However, the inconsistent development of reporting frameworks tailored to different needs has occasionally led to data overlaps. As a result, the industry has been pushing for greater coordination and data sharing between authorities in recent years to avoid data redundancies and inconsistencies, thereby streamline reporting procedures. Accordingly, the harmonisation of reporting obligations was approved as a solution to this challenge.[3]

2.1.1 European Central Bank

At the heart of the regulatory structure in the Eurozone is the European Central Bank (ECB). The ECB serves as the foundation of the Eurozone's monetary policy framework. Founded in 1998 by the Treaty of Amsterdam, the ECB was the cornerstone of the Economic and Monetary Union (EMU). The EMU is a European Union (EU) initiative aimed at integrating member states' economies through the adoption of a common currency, the Euro and coordination of monetary policy. The ECB operates independently of political influence and is governed by the Governing Council, General Council and the Executive Board, which consist of representatives from both the ECB and the National Central Banks (NCBs). The ECB is complemented by the broader institutional framework of the European System of Central Banks (ESCB), which contains the ECB and the NCBs of all EU member states, both within and outside the Eurozone.[4] Moreover, the ECB operates within the broader EU institutional framework, working closely with other European institutions such as the European Commission and the European Parliament. This collaborative approach ensures coordination in policy-making efforts and thus creates an integrated monetary policy across the EU.[5] The main task of the ECB is to formulate and implement monetary policy for the Eurozone. This includes setting interest rates, conducting open market operations, managing the money supply to maintain price stability and overseeing monetary statistics. Together with the European Banking Authority (EBA), which develops and implements a Single Rulebook (SRB), the ECB is responsible for overlooking banking regulation and supervision in the Eurozone. This harmonises regulatory standards across countries, ensuring a level playing field for banks and enhancing financial stability. Along with National Competent Authorities

[3] European Banking Authority (2021) pp. 14–16.

[4] Scheller (2006) pp. 15–30.

[5] Pinder (2018) p. 58.

(NCAs), the ECB oversees the prudential supervision of banks in the Eurozone. This involves assessing the financial health of banks, ensuring they comply with regulatory requirements to maintain financial stability (Fig. 2.1).[6]

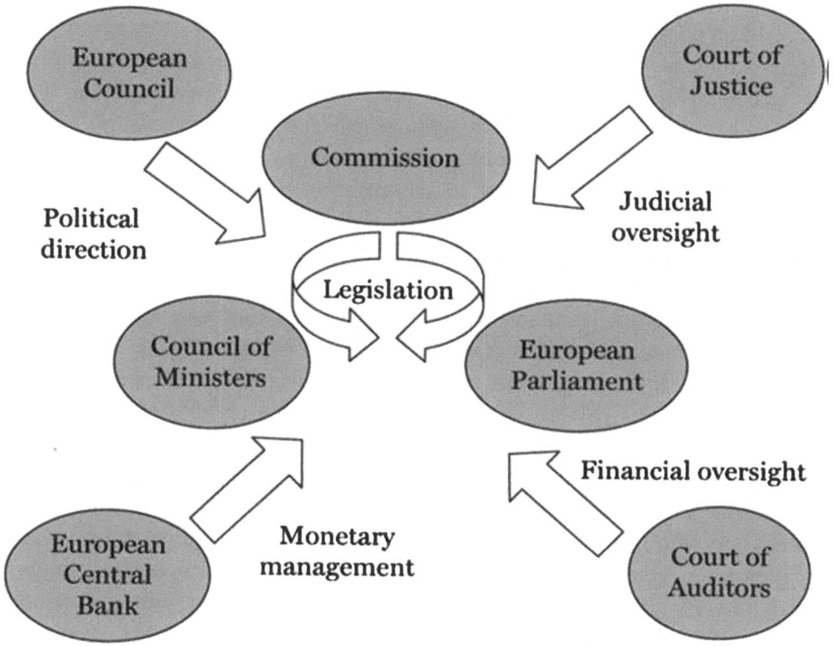

Fig. 2.1 Overview of the European Union's institutions[7]

2.1.2 Legal Framework of the EU

The legal framework within the European Union operates on a multi-tiered system, where each member state maintains its own set of laws, however, EU law prevails. The foundational treaties, such as Maastricht, Nice and Lisbon, now summarized in the Treaty on the Functioning of the European Union (TFEU)

[6] Scheller (2006) pp. 78–85.

[7] Pinder (2018) p. 58.

and Treaty on European Union (TEU), serve as primary legislation, providing the EU with the legal basis and powers. The TFEU also empowers the EU to enact secondary legislation. Secondary legislation is created to implement, interpret, or supplement the primary legislation. This can be achieved through regulations, directives and decisions, allowing for the detailed implementation and execution of EU law in specific areas.[8]

Regulations are comprehensive laws that hold immediate and direct applicability across all member states, without needing national implementation. This aspect is particularly relevant in regulatory supervision, as regulatory bodies such as the ECB and the EBA rely on EU regulations to set uniform standards and requirements for financial institutions operating in the Eurozone. For example, regulations like the Capital Requirements Regulation (CRR) form the legal framework for prudential supervision, setting out capital requirements and risk management standards that banks must adhere to. Directives serve as an order to member states, forcing them to pass legislation in line with EU objectives. While they are binding, member states retain the flexibility to choose the form of implementation. In the context of regulatory supervision, directives such as the Capital Requirements Directive IV (CRD IV) contribute to the harmonisation of regulatory practices across member states. Supervisory authorities, such as NCAs and the ECB, work together to ensure that national legislation transfers EU directives accurately. Decisions within the EU legal framework address specific issues, with the option to challenge them through judicial review. National courts act as important intermediaries between EU law and domestic legal systems, applying EU law directly and referring questions of interpretation to the European Court of Justice when necessary.[9]

Before the financial crisis, the EU pursued harmonisation to establish a single financial market. Recognizing the need for quicker responses to market changes, especially in the dynamic banking sector, the Lamfalussy procedure was introduced in the European Union. By dividing the legislative process into four levels, it allowed for more flexibility and adaptability in the law-making process for crafting financial regulations. The first two levels being more general consisting of a broad framework of directives and implementing measures, the last two levels are more detailed by focusing on technical standards and guidelines. The Lamfalussy procedure represents a significant evolution in regulatory supervision.

---

[8] Haentjens (2020) pp. 35–37.

[9] Haentjens (2020) pp. 35–41.

It builds upon earlier initiatives aimed at harmonisation and integration while introducing a more flexible approach to regulatory policymaking.[10]

2.1.3 History of Supervisory Reporting

The history of banking regulation in the EU prior to the financial crisis of 2007–2008 was characterized by a process of harmonisation and integration aimed at creating a single market for financial services. In the early years of European integration, banking regulations were primarily the responsibility of individual member states. The establishment of the European Single Market in the 1990s led to significant improvements in EU banking regulation. First directives aimed to remove barriers to cross-border banking activities.[11] The Basel Committee on Banking Supervision introduced international standards for banking regulation through the Basel Accords, which were then adopted into law by EU member states. The Basel I Accord in 1988 introduced minimum capital requirements, while Basel II, introduced in 2004, focused on risk management and capital adequacy.[12] The Financial Services Action Plan (FSAP) was established in 1999 with the goal of creating a single market for financial services in the EU. The FSAP included measures to harmonise banking regulations and to improve supervisory cooperation. Key directives under the FSAP included the Markets in Financial Instruments Directive (MiFID) and the Capital Requirements Directive (CRD). In 2004, as part of the CRD framework, the EBA introduced the Financial Reporting (FINREP) requirement, which mandated detailed financial reporting by banks. Furthermore, the CRD contained the Common Reporting (COREP) framework, established in 2006, to standardize the reporting of prudential information by banks.[13] Following the financial crisis in 2007–2008, Basel III was introduced and led to the current system of regulatory reporting. The current regulatory reporting framework consists of prudential, statistical and resolution reporting frameworks. This framework is constantly evolving and is characterised by the introduction of new reporting requirements in response to changing regulatory priorities and emerging risks within the financial sector as well as efforts to harmonise supervisory reporting.[14]

[10] Haentjens (2020) pp. 41–42.

[11] Teixeira (2017) pp. 538–541.

[12] Harnay/Scialom (2016) pp. 411–415.

[13] Teixeira (2017) pp. 541–545.

[14] Cech/Helmreich (2017) pp. 20–21.

2.1.4 De Larosière Report

In response to the 2007–2008 global financial crisis, the De Larosière Report was commissioned to identify possible improvements of the system to prevent the recurrence of such a financial crisis. It focused on financial supervision in the EU and proposed recommendations to strengthen the regulatory framework to enhance the financial stability in the European Union. One of the key recommendations was the establishment of a European System of Financial Supervisors (ESFS) to ensure harmonisation and supervision of the EU's financial system which included three new supervisory authorities: the European Banking Authority (EBA), the European Securities and Markets Authority (ESMA) and the European Insurance and Occupational Pensions Authority (EIOPA). In addition to these supervisory authorities, the European Systemic Risk Board (ESRB) was introduced. In contrast to the ESFS, which focuses on microprudential supervision at the level of individual institutions, the ESRB operates at a macroprudential level, monitoring and addressing systemic risks that could threaten the stability of the entire financial system (Fig. 2.2).[15]

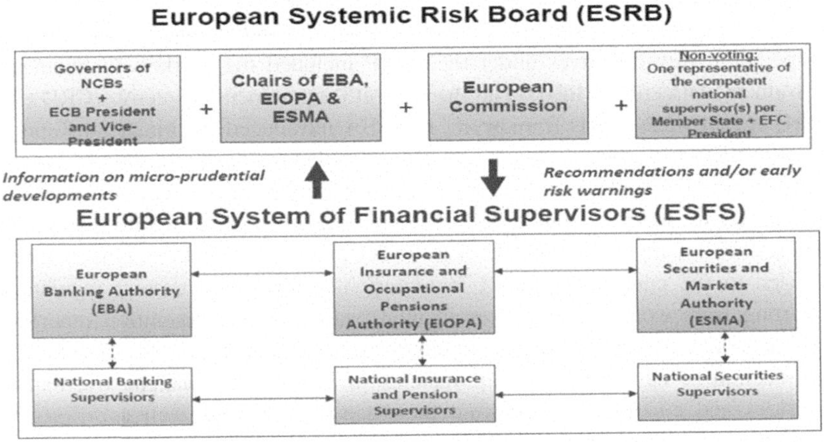

Fig. 2.2 Overview of the ESRB and ESFS[16]

---

[15] Haentjens (2020) pp. 43–44.

[16] Kaetzler/Richter (2015) p. 2.

The EBA is tasked with ensuring the effective regulation and supervision of banking institutions in the EU. Its main objectives include maintaining financial stability, protecting consumers and promoting transparency and integrity in the EU banking sector. The EBA works closely with NCAs and other EU institutions to develop regulatory standards, the Single Rulebook, conduct stress tests and produce guidelines on banking practices.[17]

ESMA is responsible for protecting the stability and integrity of financial markets in the EU. ESMA plays a vital role in regulating securities markets, ensuring investor protection and promoting market transparency. It works closely with NCAs or other EU institutions to develop harmonised regulatory standards, monitor markets and provide guidance on securities and investment practices.[18]

EIOPA main objective is to ensure the stability and integrity of the insurance and occupational pensions sectors in the EU. It works with the NCAs and other EU institutions to develop regulatory standards, carry out risk assessments and promote consumer protection in these sectors.[19]

2.1.5 Banking Union

Another important lesson learned from the financial crisis was the need for a unified banking supervision system within the EU. This realization emphasized the need to create a single regulatory framework that can effectively regulate and supervise banks operating in different member states. The Banking Union was established to centralize supervision and resolution mechanisms at the European level. The Banking Union aims to minimize the risks associated with national banking systems and prevent the spread of financial instability across borders. It is based on a three-pillar approach, which can be seen in Fig. 2.3.[20]

---

[17] Ferran (2016) pp. 286–288.

[18] Schammo (2011) pp. 1880–1883.

[19] Keune (2015) pp. 82–85.

[20] Cech/Helmreich (2017) pp. 28–29.

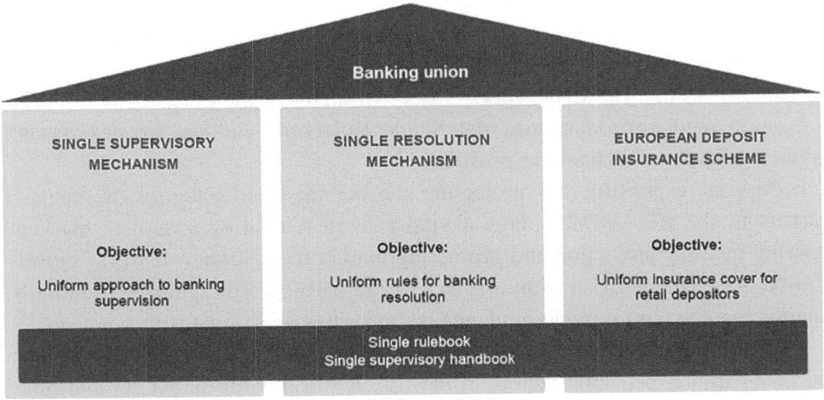

Fig. 2.3 Overview of the pillars of the Banking Union[21]

The first pillar, known as the Single Supervisory Mechanism (SSM), is designed to enhance the effectiveness of supervision while promoting cross-border cooperation and coordination. Under the SSM, the ECB is responsible for the direct supervision of significant banks, while less significant banks are supervised by the NCAs.[22] To qualify as significant, banks must meet at least one criterion in size, economic importance, cross-border activities, or direct public financial assistance (Fig. 2.4).[23]

The second pillar, the Single Resolution Mechanism (SRM), is intended to ensure the structured resolution of failing banks. The concept for the third pillar, European Deposit and Insurance Scheme (EDIS), is built upon the existing structure of national deposit guarantee schemes, which have been harmonised to ensure full coverage for all deposits across the EU, up to € 100.000 per individual and per bank.[24]

[21] Oesterreichische Nationalbank (n.d.h) n. pag.

[22] Oesterreichische Nationalbank (n.d.g) n. pag.

[23] European Central Bank (n.d.h) n. pag.

[24] Oesterreichische Nationalbank (n.d.g) n. pag.

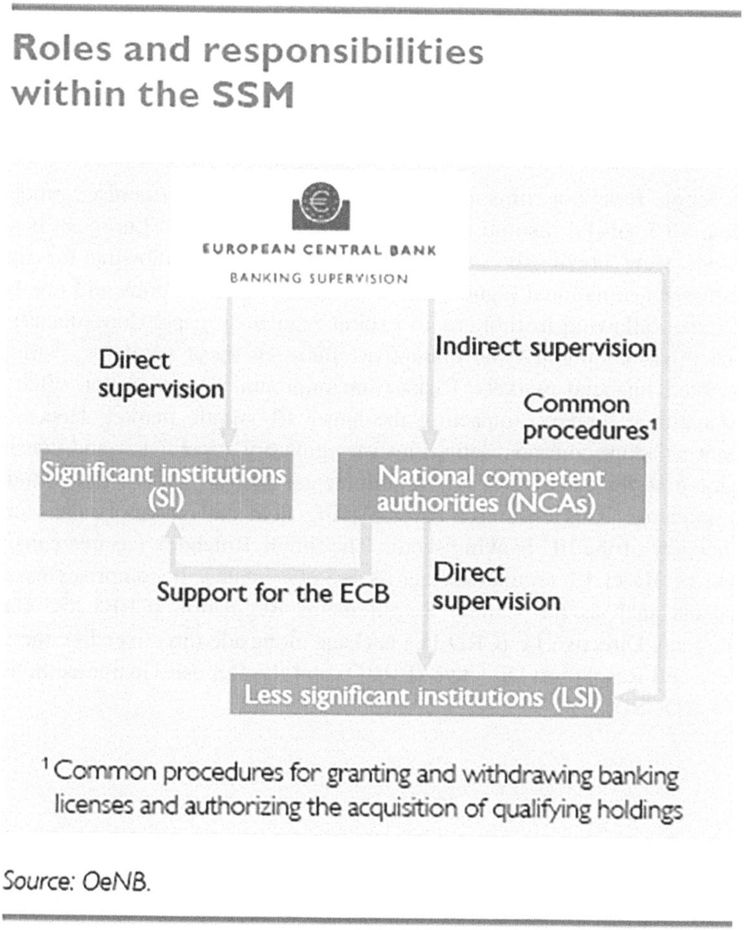

Fig. 2.4 Overview of the SSM[25]

---

[25] Oesterreichische Nationalbank (n.d.f) n. pag.

Consistency in supervisory practices within the banking union is guaranteed through the utilization of a Single Rulebook and a Single Supervisory Handbook. The ECB together with the EBA, plays a crucial role by issuing regulations, guidelines, recommendations and instructions for the banking system as a whole and is therefore accountable for ensuring the effectiveness and uniformity of the SSM.[26]

The Single Rulebook aims to establish a unified set of harmonised prudential rules that all financial institutions in the EU must adhere to. European banking regulations were previously structured around directives, allowing for significant variations in national regulations. This led to interpretations and regulatory uncertainties, allowing institutions to exploit regulatory gaps. Consequently, the financial crisis highlighted the disruptive effects of these regulatory variations in integrated financial markets. Risks from minimum harmonisation often spill beyond national borders, impacting the entire EU single market. Hence, it is important to adopt common definitions of regulatory supervision and consistent methodologies for calculating key requirements, such as capital ratios and liquidity standards. This ensures a level playing field and enhances the stability and efficiency of the EU banking sector. The Single Rulebook ensures consistent adoption of Basel III regulations across member states. It comprises essential components such as the Capital Requirements Regulation (CRR), the Capital Requirements Directive IV (CRD IV) package alongside directives like the Bank Recovery and Resolution Directive (BRRD) and the Deposit Guarantee Schemes Directive (DGSD).[27]

---

[26] Oesterreichische Nationalbank (n.d.g) n. pag.

[27] European Banking Authority (n.d.b) n. pag.

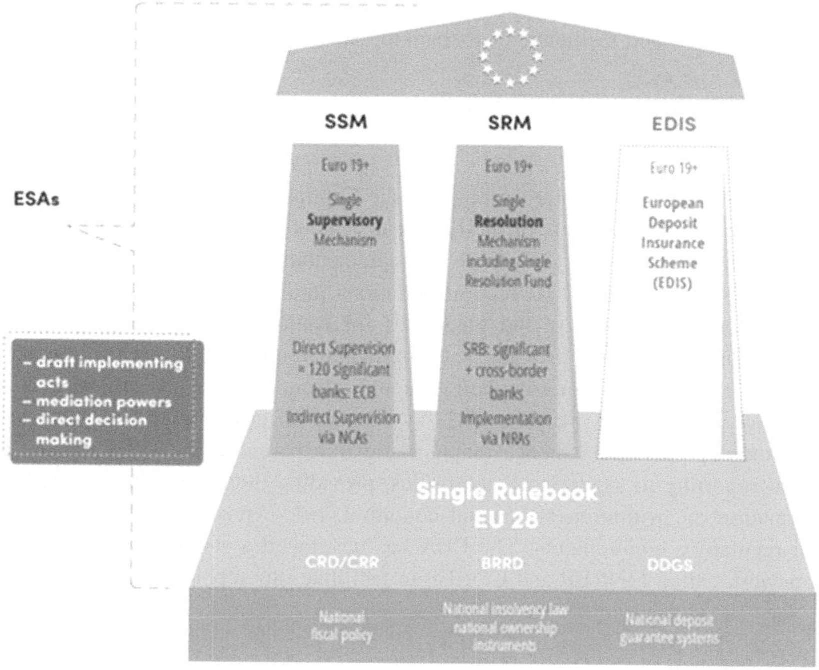

Fig. 2.5 Overview of the SRB[28]

2.2 Important Banking Regulations

As seen in Fig. 2.5, the Single Rulebook, together with the SSM, the SRM and with EDIS, provides the foundation of the Banking Union. The banking regulations CRR/CRD IV, BRRD and DGSD serve as its implementation. These directives and regulations require banks to report various financial and risk-related data to regulatory authorities such as the ECB, NCAs and EBA on a regular basis.[29] However, recognizing the need for continuous adaptation and improvement in response to evolving financial dynamics, several proposed revisions to existing regulations have emerged. The introduction of CRR II, CRR III, CRD V,

[28] Lintner et al. (2017) p. 24.

[29] Montalbano (2021) pp. 229–233.

CRD VI and BRRD II signifies the European Union's commitment to enhancing the effectiveness and resilience of its banking sector.

2.2.1 CRR / CRD IV

The Capital Requirements Regulation and the Capital Requirements Directive IV are fundamental components of the European Union's banking regulatory framework under the SSM. They serve as an implementation of the Basel III accord, as they translate the Basel III recommendations into applicable EU law, setting out prudential requirements and guidelines for banks and financial institutions operating in the EU.[30] The CRR sets prudential requirements for credit institutions, including rules for calculating capital adequacy, liquidity standards and a leverage ratio framework. The CRD IV focuses on governance, risk management and capital buffers, hence emphasizing transparency. The CRR mandates regular reporting to supervisory authorities, providing them with comprehensive information on institutions' financial condition, risk exposures and compliance with regulatory requirements. The EBA has developed a standardized reporting framework called FINREP and COREP to facilitate this reporting process.[31]

2.2.2 BRRD

The Bank Recovery and Resolution Directive is an important EU law to regulate failed banks and therefore reducing risk to the financial system. The BRRD provides the legal basis and framework for bank recovery and resolution activities within the EU, including the formation of resolution authorities in member states. The SRM regulation builds upon the principles and provisions of the BRRD, ensuring consistency and coherence in the resolution framework across the EU. It urges national decision-making authorities to develop a systematic restructuring of banks, emphasizing tools such as bailing out. Banks also need to develop recovery plans to be resilient.[32]

---

[30] European Commission (n.d.) n. pag.

[31] Masera (2014) pp. 381–383.

[32] Lintner et al. (2017) pp. 29–34.

2.2.3 DGSD

The Deposit Guarantee Scheme is a mechanism to protect depositors in the event of a bank failure and hence to maintain financial stability. The DGSD ensures a harmonised approach to deposit guarantee schemes across the EU.[33] It sets out common rules for the protection of deposits in the event of a bank failure. The DGSD establishes minimum coverage levels for deposit guarantee schemes, mandates reimbursement of depositors and outlines funding mechanisms through ex-ante contributions from banks.[34] No agreement has yet been reached on a European wide DGSD.[35]

2.3 Reporting Requirements

EU banks are obligated to report a variety of data, including statistical, resolution and prudential information. These obligations are outlined in EU legal frameworks, such as ECB regulations on balance sheet items (BSI) and interest rates (MIR), the sectoral module of Securities Holdings Statistics (SHS-S), AnaCredit for credit and credit risk data, the EBA's technical standards for supervisory data like COREP and FINREP and reporting to the Single Resolution Board. While existing ECB regulations specify the required information, they don't detail the reporting process itself, including data organization, definitions, or deadlines.[36] National central banks can collect this data under their own frameworks, which also cover reporting to the ECB for statistics not covered by ECB regulations. Additionally, national central banks fulfil reporting requirements for international organizations like the Bank for International Settlements (BIS) and the International Monetary Fund (IMF), as well as national data needs.[37] Below are brief mentions of the most important reporting frameworks relevant for the Integrated Financial Reporting Framework that will be discussed later in this thesis.

[33] Chiti (2019) pp. 392–397.

[34] Sanction Scanner (n.d.) n. pag.

[35] Goodhart/Sato (2024) p. 2.

[36] Novak/Muchna (2023) pp. 2–5.

[37] European Central Bank (2022) pp. 1–2.

2.3.1 Prudential Reporting Framework

The EBA is under the CRR responsible for the development of Binding Technical Standards (BTS), which delve into Implementation Technical Standards (ITS) and Regulatory Technical Standards (RTS). These function as legal acts e.g. a directive or regulation, that aim at ensuring consistent harmonisation in specific areas and are responsible for implementing the CRR, CRD IV, the BRRD and the DGSD. Once adopted by the European Commission, these standards become legally binding and are directly applicable across all member states. The standards cover various aspects of banking regulation, including prudential requirements, risk management, capital adequacy and resolution frameworks.[38]

Based on the EU regulation No. 680/2014 and its updated version 2022/2453, financial institutions operating in the Eurozone are subject to a comprehensive statistical, prudential and resolution reporting obligations. These regulations lay down the ITS and the RTS with regards to supervisory reporting under the CRR. ITS provides standardized forms and templates as well as reporting frequencies and reporting formats to be used by supervised banks and other financial institutions when providing information to the NCAs. The information collected through these forms is then compiled by the NCAs and submitted to relevant European Union regulatory bodies, such as ECB. RTS comprises detailed regulations addressing specific provisions with precise norms, specifications and measurement methodologies. There exists manual insertion and automated transmission of information to the NCAs. Financial institutions are required to submit standardized reports, following ITS and RTS guidelines, to regulatory authorities on a regular basis.[39] So, in summary, the CRR/CRD IV, BRRD and DGSD establish the overarching regulatory framework for banking within the EU. The EBA, as a regulatory authority, develops specific standards and frameworks such as BTS, ITS and RTS to ensure consistent and effective regulatory reporting by banks, through frameworks like COREP and FINREP.

2.3.1.1 COREP

COREP, which stands for Common Reporting, aims to increase transparency in regulatory reporting by requiring more granular data. It is enforced across the European Union and covers both credit institutions and investment firms, ensuring that a wide range of financial organisations comply with the guidelines. Through

[38] European Banking Authority (n.d.b) n. pag.

[39] Clifford (2017) p. 6.

monthly and quarterly reporting templates, COREP requires these institutions to accurately document their capital adequacy and capital requirements.[40]

The main reporting requirements of COREP templates encompass five main areas. Firstly, there's a focus on ensuring that banks and financial institutions have sufficient capital to handle any potential risks, so they are required to report their capital adequacy. Another key aspect is the assessment of the risks associated with lending, both to individuals and other institutions. This includes a thorough analysis of the potential dangers associated with the credit and counterparty credit risk. Group solvency addresses the financial stability of larger groups of institutions and ensures that they have sufficient collective capital to withstand unexpected financial difficulties. Lastly, institutions must report on market and operational risks to provide a comprehensive picture of their risk management practices.[41]

2.3.1.2 FINREP

FINREP stands for Financial Reporting and is a regulatory framework developed by the EBA for standardizing financial reporting by European banks and financial institutions. FINREP aims to enhance harmonisation and convergence in supervisory reporting requirements. It is applicable to all credit institutions that consolidate their financial reports based on International Financial Reporting Standards (IFRS).[42] FINREP can also be carried out according to nGAAP, i.e. according to national accounting regulations.[43] The FINREP templates contain a comprehensive range of financial reporting elements, including primary statements such as balance sheets and income statements. They also cover additional primary statements like comprehensive income and equity. In addition, FINREP requires the disclosure of financial assets and liabilities as well as the disclosure of financial assets and off-balance sheet activities. It also includes disclosures on non-financial instruments, providing a full overview of an institutions' financial position.[44]

---

[40] Cech/Helmreich (2017) p. 30.

[41] European Banking Authority (2011) pp. 1–5.

[42] Bellairs/Bradley (2022) n. pag.

[43] Stindt/Schönfelder (2014) pp. 652–656.

[44] Stindt/Schönfelder (2014) pp. 654–656.

2.3.2 Statistical Reporting Framework

The Directorate General Statistics of the ECB is responsible for overseeing the efficient delivery of statistical data required for various functions within the ESCB. This entails collecting, compiling and analysing a wide range of economic and financial data to support decision-making processes and ensure the accuracy and reliability of statistical reporting. Moreover, the ESCB ensures that statistical information is made available not only to policymakers, but also to market participants and the public. By using different statistical reporting frameworks, the ECB can produce comprehensive and insightful statistics that are important for maintaining market stability and managing risk.[45]

2.3.2.1 AnaCredit

AnaCredit is a regulation aimed at harmonising the collection of detailed information on individual loans and credit exposures within the Eurozone as well as establishing a common granular credit database in the Eurozone. Its primary objective is to enhance the ECB's ability to conduct monetary policy, monitor financial stability and assess credit risk accurately. Under AnaCredit, Eurozone banks are required to report granular data on their credit exposures to businesses and households, including information on borrower characteristics such as sector, size and location, loan terms such as interest rates and maturity and collateral details. The dataset covers a wide range of credit instruments, including loans, overdrafts and other forms of credit granted by banks.[46]

2.3.2.2 Balance Sheet Items

Within the framework of European regulations, NCBs routinely gather and distribute monthly data regarding balance sheet items (BSI) of monetary and financial institutions (MFIs). These BSI figures serve as fundamental inputs for generating both national and euro-area monetary aggregates and their corresponding measures. These aggregates play a significant role in the ECB's evaluation of price stability risks and in establishing minimum reserve requirements for banks in the EU. BSI typically encompasses details regarding assets, such as cash and loans, liabilities like deposits from customers and borrowings and details on equity, such as common stock or retained earnings.[47]

[45] Salou (2008) p. 313.

[46] European Central Bank (n.d.d) pp. 1–10.

[47] Cusano et al. (2021) p. 7.

2.3.2.3 Interest Rates of Monetary Financial Institutions

The monetary financial institution (MIR) interest rate statistics cover all interest rates applied by euro area resident credit institutions to euro-denominated deposits and loans to all households and non-financial corporations' resident in the participating EU member states.[48] The interest rates and volumes for the euro area are calculated and collected monthly. These statistics play a crucial role in the assessment of the impact of monetary policy on the euro area economy, regarding the extent and speed with which policy rates and market interest rates influence lending and deposit rates for households and non-financial corporations.[49]

2.3.2.4 Securities Holdings Statistics

Securities holdings statistics (SHS-S) refer to a set of data collected and compiled by central banks or other regulatory authorities to provide information on the securities holdings of different sectors of the economy. These statistics provide insights into the composition, ownership and distribution of securities within a particular country or region. The SHS-S typically covers a wide range of securities, including shares, bonds, money market instruments and other financial instruments held by various sectors such as households, non-financial corporations, financial institutions and government agencies. Data collection for the SHS-S can be regular, e.g. quarterly, or annually, depending on the reporting requirements and the frequency of updates needed for analyses and policy decisions. The main purpose of the SHS-S is to provide policy makers, researchers and analysts with comprehensive information on the structure and dynamics of securities holdings in the economy. These statistics can be used to monitor trends in investment behavior, to assess risks to financial stability and to formulate appropriate policy measures.[50]

2.3.3 Resolution Reporting Framework

Reporting to the Single Resolution Board (SRB) is a key aspect of the European banking supervision framework, which was introduced as part of the SSM. The SRB sets out specific reporting requirements. These requirements cover a wide

[48] European Central Bank (n.d.f) n. pag.

[49] Feraboli et al. (2015) pp. 2–3.

[50] Boermans (2022) pp. 5–7.

range of financial and supervisory data, including balance sheet data, risk positions, capital ratios, liquidity ratios and other relevant metrics. Reporting to the SRB generally takes place on a regular basis, with the frequency of reporting determined by the SRB based on the size, complexity and risk profile of the supervised institutions. Reporting deadlines are set to ensure the timely provision of data to support effective supervision and risk management. The SRB uses this information to assess the financial situation, risk profile and compliance status of supervised institutions, to identify emerging risks or vulnerabilities and to take appropriate supervisory action where necessary.[51]

2.3.4 Other Reporting Requirements

Within the European supervisory framework, there are numerous reporting requirements that are essential for maintaining financial transparency and regulatory supervision, the list of which is beyond the scope of this paper. Some other relevant supervisory reporting frameworks include the collection and analysis of balance of payments data and international investment position statistics. These datasets provide an understanding of a country's economic transactions with the rest of the world, including trade in goods and services, financial flows and international investment positions. Another important reporting obligation concerns Securities Issuance Statistics. This involves the systematic collection and verification of data relating to the issuance of securities such as shares, bonds and other financial instruments.[52]

In addition, national requirements play a crucial role in the supervisory framework and include several reporting obligations imposed by national authorities. These requirements may include the submission of data for credit registers or housing market statistics to supervisory authorities or other relevant institutions.[53]

---

[51] Single Resolution Board (2024) n. pag.

[52] Pinheiro (2014) pp. 2–4.

[53] Oesterreichische Nationalbank (n.d.e) n. pag.

2.4 Technical Aspects of Reporting

2.4.1 Database Systems

In today's dynamic business landscape, managing data efficiently is crucial for organizations navigating supervisory reporting requirements. Efficient data management often relies on the utilization of a computer database. A database serves as a centralized computer system that enables the user to store, retrieve and update a variety of related data, crucial for meeting supervisory reporting obligations. A database has two types of data such as end-user data and metadata. End-user data encompasses the raw facts or information relevant to the end user. Metadata refers to data about data, facilitating the integration and management of end-user data within the database. A database management system (DBMS) comprises a collection of programs responsible for managing the structure of the database and regulating access to the stored data. Hence, a database is the information to be stored, DBMS provides the system to manage the database.[54]

The DBMS functions as the intermediary between the user and the database, serving as a bridge that facilitates access to the database structure stored as a collection of files. Accessing data in these files is only possible through the DBMS. All application requests are routed through the DBMS, which then translates them into the complex operations necessary to fulfill those requests. By doing so, the DBMS hides the application programs and users from much of the database's internal complexity.[55]

The DBMS allows users to define the structure of the database, including specifying the types of data that can be stored, the relationships between different data elements and any constraints or rules that must be enforced. DBMS provides tools for users to manipulate the data stored in the database, such as adding, modifying, deleting and querying records. This is typically done through a query language like Structured Query Language (SQL) (Fig. 2.6).[56]

[54] Coronel/Morris (2019) pp. 6–8.

[55] Coronel/Morris (2019) pp. 7–8.

[56] Chopra (2010) pp. 16–18.

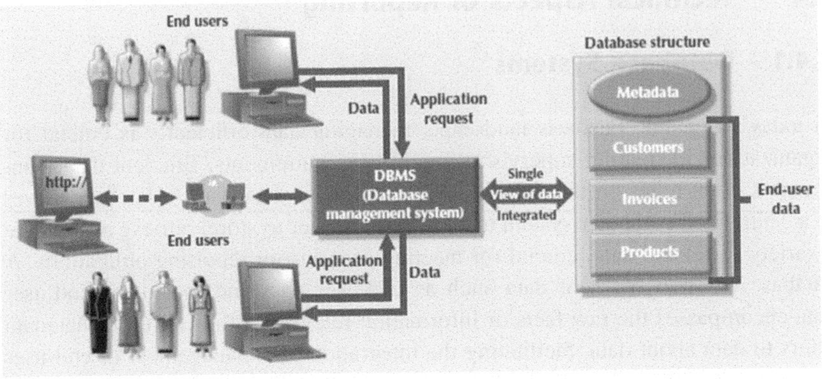

Fig. 2.6 Functionality of DBMS[57]

2.4.2 Metadata

2.4.2.1 Data Dictionary

The DBMS stores data element definitions and their relationships, known as metadata, in a data dictionary. By using the data dictionary, the DBMS finds the required data structures and relationships, eliminating the need for manual coding. Moreover, any changes made to the database structure are automatically documented in the data dictionary, freeing users from having to update all programs accessing the changed structure. The data dictionary contains definitions, descriptions and attributes of data elements, such as tables, columns, relationships, constraints and data types. The data dictionary serves as a reference for data management, providing users and systems with information about the structure and organization of the data. It helps to ensure consistency, accuracy and integrity of the data by providing a standardized source of metadata for everyone accessing the database.[58] Additionally, the data dictionary can also be used to facilitate data analysis, data integration and data governance initiatives within an organization.The Banks' Integrated Reporting Dictionary (BIRD) can be considered a specialized form of a data dictionary, customized for the banking domain.[59]

[57] Coronel/Morris (2019) p. 7.

[58] Coronel/Morris (2019) p. 24.

[59] Blaschke/Witt (2018) p. 8.

2.4.3 Data Modeling

DBMS design is centered around determining how the database structure will efficiently store and manage end-user data. At the beginning of the design process is data modeling, which creates a specific data model for a determined problem domain. A data model serves as a simplified representation, usually represented graphically, where data structures, characteristics and relations are shown.[60]

2.4.3.1 Types of Data Models

The initial aspect of data structure is often addressed within the design of a data model. There are three phases of model designing, such as conceptual data models, logical data models (LDM) and physical data models (PDM).[61] The conceptual level focuses on conveying concepts to users regarding the program's domain, outlining entities and relationships within the model's scope. It describes the semantics also referred to as the meanings or interpretation of data elements (Fig. 2.7).[62]

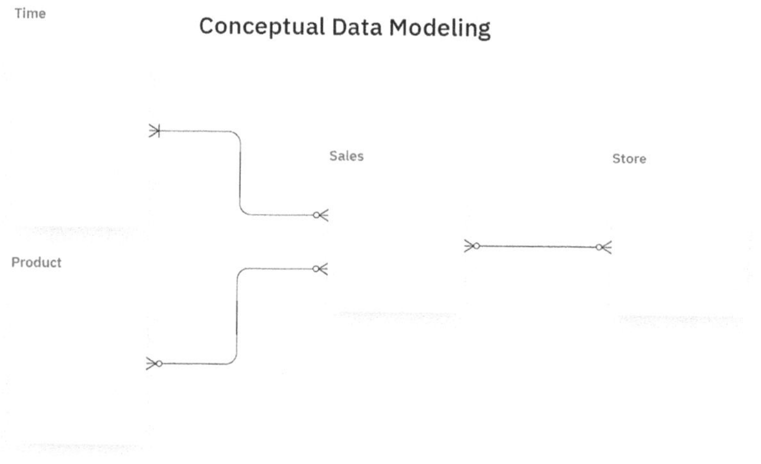

Fig. 2.7 Conceptual data modeling[63]

[60] Coronel/Morris (2019) p. 35.
[61] Mostajabi et al. (2021) p. 2.
[62] Mostajabi et al. (2021) p. 2.
[63] IBM (n.d.) n. pag.

The logical level delves deeper, communicating concepts to designers regarding the application domain with greater detail than the preceding level. The LDM serves as a blueprint, designing the structure of the database system by introducing data elements and connections between them (Fig. 2.8).[64]

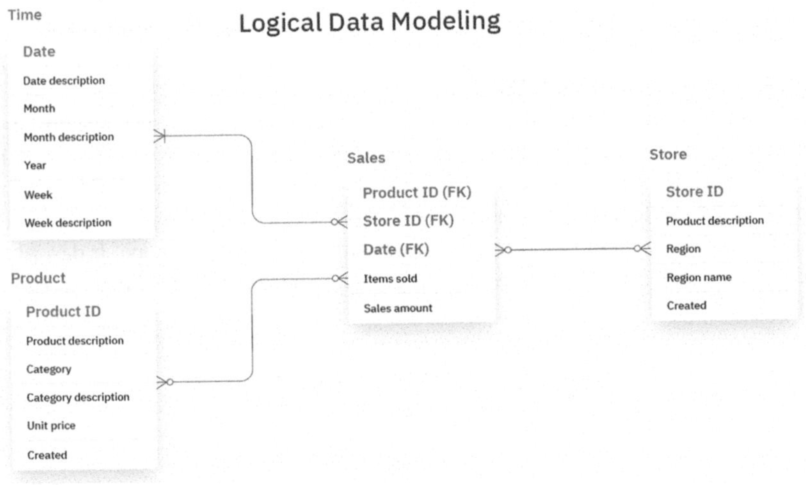

Fig. 2.8 Logical data modeling[65]

The physical level refers to the physical storage and practical implementation within a database management system, thus the logical design is translated into the physical data model by transforming entities into tables, attributes into columns and domains into data types and constraints (Fig. 2.9).[66]

[64] Mostajabi et al. (2021) p. 2.
[65] IBM (n.d.) n. pag.
[66] Mostajabi et al. (2021) p. 2.

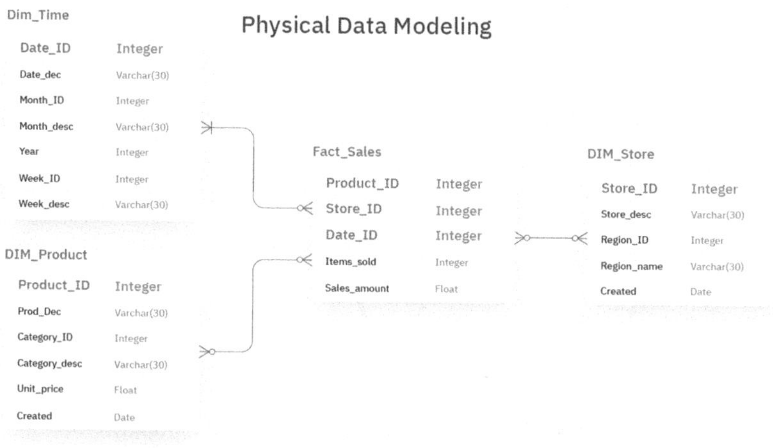

Fig. 2.9 Physical data modeling[67]

2.4.3.2 Basic Building Blocks of Data Modeling

The building blocks of all data models comprises attributes, entities, relationships and constraints. These can be seen as the foundation of the data models and are used to represent the underlying data. An entity represents a distinct element in the real world, whether it's a person, place, thing, or event for which data can be stored. Each entity is unique and identifiable. For instance, a customer entity encompasses individual customers like John Smith or Tom Strickland. Entities can range from tangible objects like customers or products to abstract concepts like flight routes or musical concerts. Attributes are associated with entities as they define the characteristics or properties of these entities. For example, attributes of a customer entity might include last name, first name, phone number, address and credit limit. Relationships describe the associations between entities. For instance, a relationship exists between customers and agents, where an agent can serve multiple customers and each customer can be served by one agent. Data models typically employ three types of relationships: one-to-many, many-to-many and one-to-one. These relationships are often denoted using shorthand notations like 1:M, M:N and 1:1, respectively (Fig. 2.10).[68]

---

[67] IBM (n.d.) n. pag.

[68] Coronel/Morris (2019) pp. 36–37.

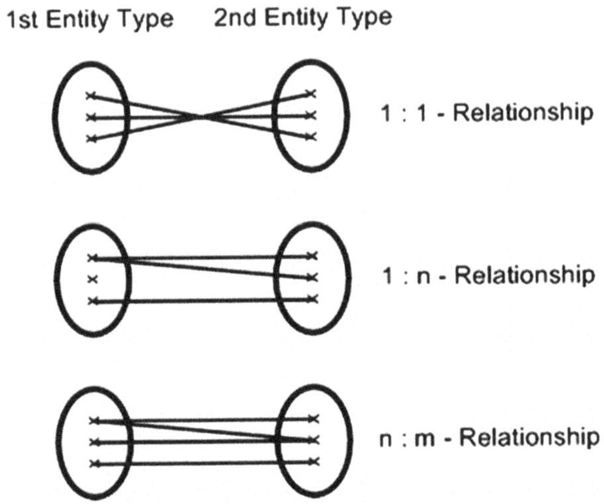

Fig. 2.10 Relationships in data modeling[69]

One-to-many (1:M) relationships show that one entity instance is associated with multiple instances of another entity. For example, a customer may generate multiple invoice instances, but each invoice is generated by only one customer. Many-to-many (M:N) relationships indicate that multiple instances of one entity are associated with multiple instances of another entity.[70] A student can enroll in multiple class instances and each class can have multiple students. One-to-one (1:1) relationships denote a unique association between two entities. For instance, in a retail company, each store may be managed by one employee and each employee manages only one store.[71]

2.4.4 Designing of a Data Model

When designing a database, an entity-relationship model (ERM) is often created first to capture the conceptual structure of the data to be stored and the relationships between the entities. This ERM serves as a blueprint for understanding the

---

[69] WU Wien (n.d.) n. pag.

[70] Coronel/Morris (2019) p. 37.

[71] SAP (2023) n. pag.

organization of the data. Once the ERM is designed, the next step is to translate this conceptual or logical model into a relational model (RM) for practical implementation. The RM focuses on the actual organization of data in tables consisting of rows and columns. By converting the ERM into a RM, a concrete framework is created for setting up the database structure. The relational model derived from the ERM serves as the foundation for setting up the database structure used in supervisory reporting systems. Data collected from financial institutions, market participants and other sources can be stored and organized according to the relational model, facilitating efficient data retrieval, analysis and reporting. For the development of the OeNB's Basic Cube an ERM was used and will be provided later as an example.

2.4.4.1 Entity Relationship Model

An ERM serves as a conceptual while an entity-relationship diagram (ERD) visually illustrates the relationships between entities within a system or database. It is a crucial step in the process of database design as it helps to organize and understand the structure of data and how different pieces of information relate to each other. ERMs are often used as a precursor to the actual implementation of a database, serving as a blueprint for creating the physical database schema. ERM is considered a logical data model and consists of the basic building blocks described earlier as well as cardinality and keys.[72] Each entity is represented by a rectangle in the ERM diagram. For example, in a university database, entities could include students, courses and professors. Relationships are typically represented by lines connecting the relevant entities. A diamond shape is placed along the line to indicate the relation.[73] Cardinality is indicated using symbols near the ends of the relationship lines. In an ERM, keys are attributes or combinations of attributes that uniquely identify instances of an entity within a database. Keys are typically indicated within the entity rectangles in an ERD. For example, a "student" entity might have a primary key attribute "student ID" underlined to signify its importance in uniquely identifying students. Additionally, there are weak entities, that are entities that cannot be uniquely identified by their attributes alone (Fig. 2.11).[74]

---

[72] Halpin (2008) pp. 306–310.

[73] Halpin (2008) pp. 306–310.

[74] Halpin (2008) pp. 306–310.

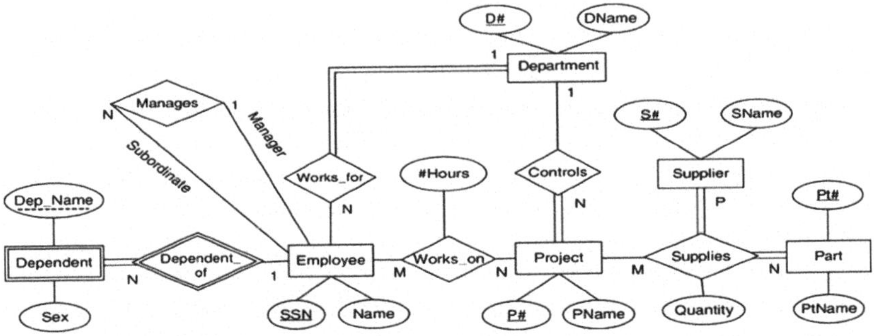

Fig. 2.11 Example of an ERD[75]

2.4.5 Data Models in Supervisory Reporting

In financial reporting, the quality of the data and timeliness of business information are essential, as well as the speed of collection and formation of the information reported. Under the ITS, the EBA develops supervisory reporting frameworks, such as FINREP or COREP. To effectively process the reported data, the EBA introduced the Data Point Model (DPM). This abstract data model involves specifying data points through numerous parameters, each with different characteristics. The combination of these parameters and their traits delineates a singular data point, to which a value can be attributed. Comprehensive tables or templates can be generated by combining these data points. Functional specifications are presented in Excel format as tables. However, these specifications are exclusively transmitted in eXtensible Business Reporting Language (XBRL) format, rather than in their original Excel form.[76]

---

[75] Liu/Özsu (2009) p. 1319.

[76] Sutterer (2021) n. pag.

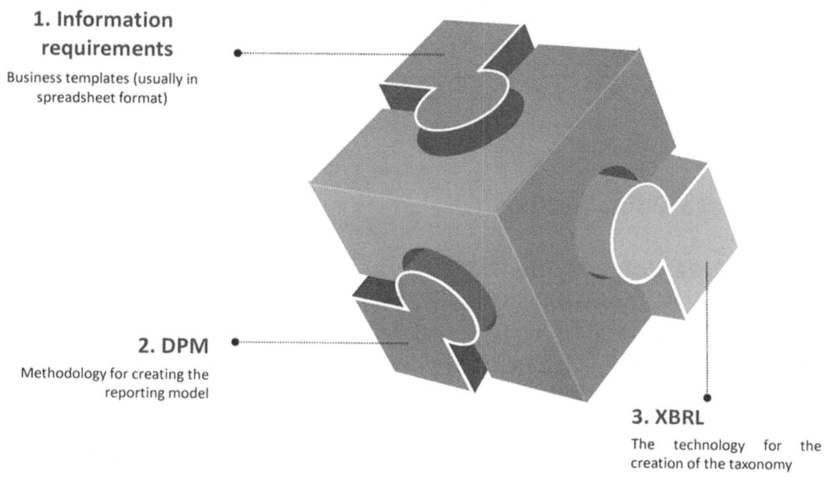

Fig. 2.12 Technical aspects of supervisory reporting[77]

Illustrated in Fig. 2.12 is the process of supervisory reporting with data models. It starts with the EBA that defines the reporting requirements for banks. These requirements encompass a wide range of financial data, such as prudential, statistical or resolution reporting. The EBA develops the DPM, which serves as a standardized framework for organizing and representing the reporting requirements, hence connecting the templates to the XBRL taxonomy. The DPM includes a set of data points, each representing a specific piece of information that must be reported by financial institutions. The FINREP/COREP or AnaCredit templates are standardized reporting templates that align with the reporting requirements specified by the EBA. These templates are based on the DPM and provide a structured format for financial institutions to report their data. Each data point in the DPM corresponds to a specific cell or field in the FINREP/COREP or AnaCredit templates. Financial institutions map their internal financial data to the templates based on the Data Point Model. This mapping ensures that the data reported by banks aligns with the standardized reporting requirements set by the EBA. Financial institutions convert their mapped data from the templates into XBRL format for submission to the regulatory authorities. Upon receiving the reports, regulatory authorities validate the data to ensure its accuracy, completeness and compliance with FINREP / COREP or AnaCredit requirements. This

[77] Mora (2020) p. 3.

validation process may involve automated checks and manual review to identify any discrepancies or errors in the reported data. Once validated, the data is processed to generate aggregated reports and analyses for regulatory oversight purposes.

2.4.6 Data Point Model

2.4.6.1 Data Point Modelling

In the context of supervisory reporting, Data Point Modelling is a methodology for the development of financial data models that describe characteristics of the information exchanged within supervisory reporting processes. These models are commonly known as Data Point Models or as meta-data and are represented through XBRL taxonomy files.[78] Data Point Modelling tries to create a bridge between a reporting framework, the reporting templates and the technical design of an XBRL taxonomy.[79] They provide a technical implementation of the reporting requirements, so the ITS have been translated into a DPM.[80] Each data point in the DPM is identified by a unique code and includes information about its attributes, relationships and validation rules.[81] A data point can be described in textual documentation or by a cell in the tabular format of a data model and represents a data requirement that financial institutions have to report. Data requirements described as a series of tables and supporting text documents serve as the basis of the reporting process. The reportable data requires the combination of information, such as financial standards, regulations, the required information in the tables and supportive documentation. The outcome of each data point results in a complete set of data points explicitly described, enabling the identification of relationships between them across different tables or documentation sections.[82] The relationships are depicted by validation rules, which consist of formulas or expressions determining whether the value of a given data point meets the criteria or not. To facilitate the consistent use of ITS in supervisory reporting, EBA provides the DPM and XBRL classifications. For the DPM, these are comprehensive guidelines, describing the content of each data point. Additionally, it establishes all relevant business concepts, relationships and

[78] European Banking Authority (2014) p. 4.

[79] Eurofiling (n.d.) n. pag.

[80] Rossi/Gillet (2020) p. 4.

[81] European Banking Authority (2014) pp. 4–10.

[82] Eurofiling (2009) pp. 3–4.

rules together with the classification. XBRL classifications define dictionaries of reportable information.[83] The DPM converts the templates into a readable table format.

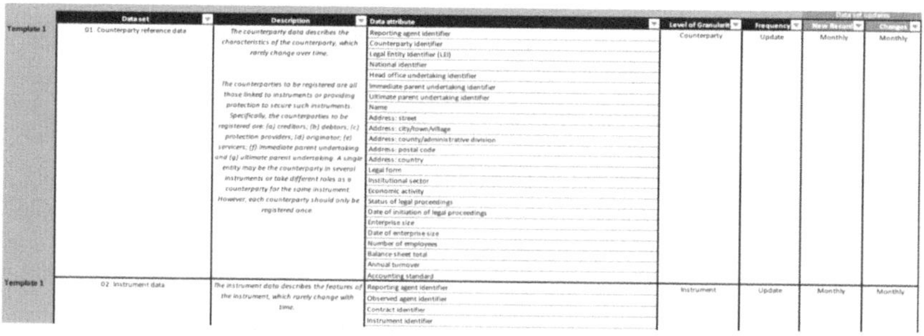

	Data set	Description	Data attribute	Level of Granularit	Frequency	New Record	Changes
Template 1	01 Counterparty reference data	The counterparty data describes the characteristics of the counterparty, which rarely change over time. The counterparties to be registered are all those linked to instruments or providing protection to secure such instruments. Specifically, the counterparties to be registered are: (a) creditors; (b) debtors; (c) protection providers; (d) originator; (e) servicers; (f) immediate parent undertaking and (g) ultimate parent undertaking. A single entity may be the counterparty in several instruments or take different roles as a counterparty for the same instrument. However, each counterparty should only be registered once.	Reporting agent identifier Counterparty identifier Legal Entity Identifier (LEI) National identifier Head office undertaking identifier Immediate parent undertaking identifier Ultimate parent undertaking identifier Name Address: street Address: city/town/village Address: county/administrative division Address: postal code Address: country Legal form Institutional sector Economic activity Status of legal proceedings Date of initiation of legal proceedings Enterprise size Date of enterprise size Number of employees Balance sheet total Annual turnover Accounting standard	Counterparty	Update	Monthly	Monthly
Template 1	02 Instrument data	The instrument data describes the features of the instrument, which rarely change with time.	Reporting agent identifier Observed agent identifier Contract identifier Instrument identifier	Instrument	Update	Monthly	Monthly

Fig. 2.13 AnaCredit reporting template[84]

Figure 2.14 shows the AnaCredit template from Fig. 2.13 converted into the DPM.

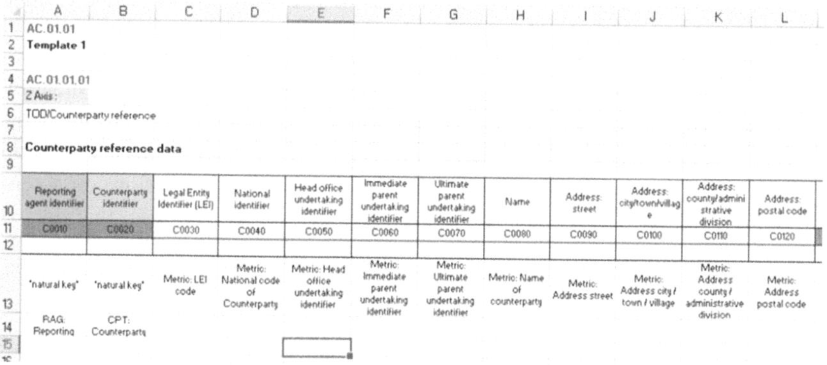

	A	B	C	D	E	F	G	H	I	J	K	L
1	AC.01.01											
2	**Template 1**											
3												
4	AC.01.01.01											
5	Z Axis:											
6	TOD/Counterparty reference											
7												
8	**Counterparty reference data**											
9												
10	Reporting agent identifier	Counterparty identifier	Legal Entity Identifier (LEI)	National identifier	Head office undertaking identifier	Immediate parent undertaking identifier	Ultimate parent undertaking identifier	Name	Address: street	Address: city/town/village	Address: county/administrative division	Address: postal code
11	C0010	C0020	C0030	C0040	C0050	C0060	C0070	C0080	C0090	C0100	C0110	C0120
12												
13	"natural key"	"natural key"	Metric: LEI code	Metric: National code of Counterparty	Metric: Head office undertaking identifier	Metric: Immediate parent undertaking identifier	Metric: Ultimate parent undertaking identifier	Metric: Name of counterparty	Metric: Address street	Metric: Address city / town / village	Metric: Address county / administrative division	Metric: Address postal code
14	RAG: Reporting	CPT: Counterparty										
15												

Fig. 2.14 DPM for AnaCredit template[85]

[83] Romano et al. (2021) pp. 7–8.

[84] XBRL (2021) n. pag.

[85] XBRL (2021) n. pag.

To illustrate how the concept is embedded in the definition, an example of a specific data point is provided. The data point "Total assets" is denoted by the XBRL metric XBRL:MET(EBA:mi53) and the context EBA:BAS(×6)EBA:MCY(×25), where:[86]

- "mi53" signifies "Carrying amount" measured in monetary units [m] and categorized as a stock [i];
- "BAS" explains the fundamental conceptual essence of the data point and identifies the framework within which it's situated. The addition of "×6" specifically identifies the value as pertaining to "Assets";
- "MCY" delineates the underlying concept being reported, with the value "x25" specifying "Total assets".

2.4.7 Validation Rules

Validation rules serve as checks applied to reported data to ensure its consistency. If a validation rule applied to a set of data yields true, the reported data is consistent according to that rule. However, if the result is false, it indicates an inconsistency in the reported information that requires checking or correction. These rules are formulated based on a set of variables that are bound to reported data during the validation process. The data to which a variable should be bound is determined by filters, which allow for verification of any properties of the concepts defined in the dictionary. The scope of data, to which a validation rule is applied, can be constrained using two mechanisms: filters and preconditions. Filters associated with validation rules limit the dataset where a validation applies, while preconditions are logical expressions verifying conditions on potentially applied data. If the result of a precondition expression is false, that data is skipped.[87,88]

---

[86] Romano et al. (2021) p. 8.

[87] European Banking Authority (2014) p. 16.

[88] European Central Bank (2024b) p. 6.

2.4.7.1 Example of Validation Rules[89]


```
{    "table": "PRTY",
"type": "IF",
"attr": "TYP_PRTY",     "comparator": "!=",
   "entities":
      {
"19": "Self-employed natural person",
       "18": "Non-self-employed natural person"        },
     "value": "LST_NM",
   "originalValueName": "Last name",
   "assertComparator": "=",
   "assertValue": [
    "NULL"    ] }
```


According to this rule, in table PRTY, whenever the column TYP_PRTY is not equal to SLF_EMPLYD_NTRL_PRSN or NN_SLF_EMPLYD_NTRL_PRSN, the column LST_NM must be NULL.[90]

2.4.8 XBRL

The eXtensible Business Reporting Language aims to modernize reporting processes, eliminating human intervention and facilitating online transmission from companies to supervisory bodies. By adopting XBRL, reporting entities can report only to national supervisors. Given Europe's diverse nature, XBRL serves as a powerful tool to create a single channel of reporting. The transparency directive 2004/109 EU required the establishment of an electronic network between the national level and the national securities regulators, as well as an electronic platform across member states. Since 2008 COREP and FINREP must be reported in the XBRL format.[91]

---

[89] European Central Bank (2024) p. 3.

[90] European Central Bank (2024) p. 3.

[91] Singerová (2015) pp. 134–138.

XBRL serves as a standardized method for creating, transmitting and processing business data, particularly in business reporting. XBRL is a programming language based on XML (Extensible Markup Language) and facilitates the work with data from financial databases.[92] The international XBRL initiative emerged primarily due to shortcomings in comparability of information within financial business reporting, alongside inefficiencies in exchanging necessary data among different application systems. This push towards international XBRL adoption was driven by the need for harmonising accounting standards globally. XBRL enables the description of data structures in a more efficient manner compared to widely used formats like HTML or PDF. These traditional formats lack the ability to provide content descriptions alongside data, making processing, exchange and analysis challenging. In contrast, XBRL allows for the individual representation of both content and structure within a file.[93]

For understanding the underlying XBRL technology, two concepts, such as taxonomy and instance document, are fundamental. A taxonomy serves as standardized dictionaries or frameworks, that translate business requirements into XBRL format and contain definitions of reportable requirements. They define the elements and relationships used to represent financial data, such as assets, liabilities and equity within a hierarchical framework. This classification can cover a broad spectrum, such as places, events and more. In the context of accounting, for instance, cash falls under current assets, which in turn belongs to total assets. Additionally, a taxonomy can be represented as an XML schema. Once the taxonomy is established, the data is mapped to the taxonomy, resulting in an instance document containing tagged data in XML format. These instant documents thus encompass all essential details, including currency type and monetary values.[94] The textual instructions for reporting financial information can be translated and organized into a tabular format. As an illustration, a crucial component of the Guidelines on Financial Reporting outlined by the FINREP or COREP network consists of tables and accompanying documentation. This collection of tables and supporting documentation serves as the data model, laying the foundation for the creation of the taxonomy.[95] Taxonomies for financial reporting encompass various standards, such as the International Financial Reporting Standards (IFRS) or the United States Generally Accepted Accounting Principles (US-GAAP). In Europe, XBRL has been integrated into regulatory reporting frameworks like COREP and

[92] Plumlee/Plumlee (2008) pp. 8–10.

[93] Wolle (2014) pp. 67–69.

[94] Richards et al. (2006) p. 2.

[95] Eurofiling (2009) p. 3.

FINREP, facilitating standardized data exchange and reporting under regulatory mandates. Taxonomies are developed and maintained by standard-setting bodies like the IFRS Foundation or national regulatory authorities.[96]

To demonstrate the XBRL language, a financial statement of the XBRL International Inc. (XII) was used as an example (Fig. 2.15):[97]

ASSETS	2011		2010	
CURRENT ASSETS:				
Cash and equivalents	$ 721,596	2	624,658	1
Dues receivable	369,262	4	332,680	3
Contributions receivable	-		50,000	3
Co-sponsorship conference fees receivable, net of allowance	53,353	4	9,595	3
Investments	21,253	7,8	16,800	5,6
Prepaid expenses and other assets	7,193	10	11,080	9
Total Current Assets	1,172,657		1,044,813	

Fig. 2.15 Financial statement of XII[98]

The numbers highlighted in red indicate the line where the original financial item has been tagged according to the US GAAP 2011 XBRL taxonomy (Fig. 2.16).

label	us-gaap:Cash
⊞ contextRef	c001
⊞ unitRef	u001
decimals	0
precision	
xsi:nil	false
value	624.658

Cash	1	c001	USD	0	624.658
Cash	2	c002	USD	0	721.596
Accounts Receivable, Net, Current	3	c001	USD	0	392.275
Accounts Receivable, Net, Current	4	c002	USD	0	422.615
Other Short-term Investments	5	c001	USD	0	16.800
Short-term Investments	6	c001	USD	0	16.800
Other Short-term Investments	7	c002	USD	0	21.253
Short-term Investments	8	c002	USD	0	21.253
Prepaid Expense and Other Assets, Current	9	c001	USD	0	11.080
Prepaid Expense and Other Assets, Current	10	c002	USD	0	7.193

Fig. 2.16 Financial statement in XBRL taxonomy[99]

In the US GAAP 2011 taxonomy, "Cash" corresponds to the XII financial statement "Cash and equivalents." Similarly, lines 9 and 10, tagged as "Prepaid Expense and Other Assets, Current," map to the XII financial statement "Prepaid expense and other assets." For lines 5 and 7, the US GAAP 2011 tag is "Other

[96] Wolle (2014) pp. 67–69.

[97] Boixo (2012) p. 3.

[98] Boixo (2012) p. 3.

[99] Boixo (2012) p. 3.

Short-term Investments," while lines 6 and 8 are tagged as "Short-term Investments." Both tags represent the same XII financial statement, "Investments." Regarding lines 3 and 4, they are tagged as "Accounts Receivable, Net, Current," representing the sum of the XII financial statement items "Dues receivable," "Contributions receivable," and "Co-sponsorship conference fees receivable, net of allowance."[100]

Example of the XBRL document:[101]

```
<xbrli:context id="c001">
<xbrli:entity><xbrli:identifier scheme="www.xbrl.org">XII</...></...>
<xbrli:period><xbrli:instant>2010-06-30</...> </...></...>
<xbrli:context id="c002">
<xbrli:entity><xbrli:identifier scheme="www.xbrl.org">XII</...> </...>
<xbrli:period><xbrli:instant>2011-06-30</...> </...></...>
<xbrli:unit id="u001"> <xbrli:measure>iso4217:USD</...> </...>

<us-gaap:Cash contextRef="c001" unitRef="u001">624658</...>
<us-gaap:Cash contextRef="c002" unitRef="u001">721596</...>
<us-gaap:AccountsReceivableNetCurrent contextRef="c001" unitRef="u001">392275</...>
<us-gaap:AccountsReceivableNetCurrent contextRef="c002" unitRef="u001">422615</...>
<us-gaap:OtherShortTermInvestments contextRef="c001" unitRef="u001">16800</...>
<us-gaap:ShortTermInvestments contextRef="c001" unitRef="u001">16800</...>
<us-gaap:OtherShortTermInvestments contextRef="c002" unitRef="u001">21253</...>
<us-gaap:ShortTermInvestments contextRef="c002" unitRef="u001">21253</...>
<us-gaap:PrepaidExpenseAndOtherAssetsCurrent contextRef="c001" unitRef="u001">11080</...>
<us-gaap:PrepaidExpenseAndOtherAssetsCurrent contextRef="c002" unitRef="u001">7193</...>
```

Each snippet represents financial data for different periods (c001 for 2010–06-30 and c002 for 2011–06-30) for a certain entity ("XII"). In XBRL "u001" refers to the unit identifier. It specifies the unit in which the numerical values are expressed. In the provided context, "u001" represents the unit of measurement for the financial values, which is specified as "United States Dollar". In the provided XBRL snippets, the <us-gaap:PrepaidExpenseAndOtherAssetsCurrent> element represents a financial item related to prepaid expenses and other current assets, as defined by the US GAAP.

An illustration of the XBRL language in a European context is provided using a screenshot from AnaCredit reporting across various countries. It underscores the challenges of non-integrated reporting by highlighting discrepancies in reporting practices. Specifically, the varying definitions of "number of employees" across different countries lead to inconsistencies in reporting (Fig. 2.17).

[100] Boixo (2012) pp. 3–4.

[101] Boixo (2012) p. 4.

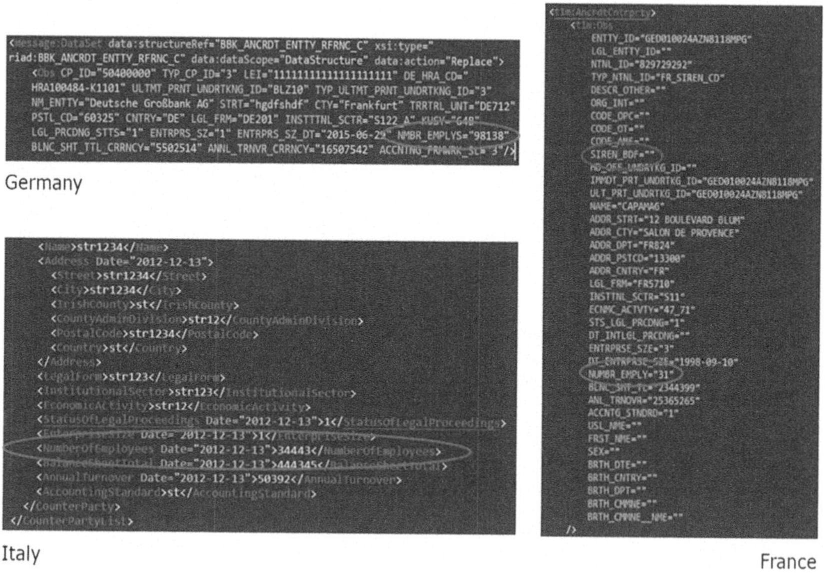

Fig. 2.17 Differences in AnaCredit reporting[102]

2.4.9 SDMX Information Model

The Statistical Data and Metadata eXchange (SDMX) is a syntax for the exchange and processing of statistical data and metadata at the ECB. Examples include data related to national accounts, such as gross domestic product, inflation rates, unemployment rates, government expenditure and trade balances.[103]

Example from OECD reporting of Australia and Austria on the quarterly reporting of gross domestic product:[104]

[102] XBRL (2021) n. pag.

[103] European Central Bank/Banco de Espana (2019) pp. 6–8.

[104] StatSilk (2021) n. pag.

```
<OECD:Series LOCATION="AUS" SUBJECT="B1_GE" MEASURE="VOBARSA"
FREQUENCY="Q" TIME_FORMAT="P3M" UNIT="AUD" POWERCODE="6"
REFERENCEPERIOD="2010">

<OECD:Obs TIME="2009-Q2" OBS_VALUE="1326162.856664"/>
<OECD:Obs TIME="2009-Q3" OBS_VALUE="1329814.001238"/>
<OECD:Obs TIME="2009-Q4" OBS_VALUE="1339180.312553"/>
<OECD:Obs TIME="2010-Q1" OBS_VALUE="1345799.681242"/>

</OECD:Series>
<OECD:Series LOCATION="AUT" SUBJECT="B1_GE" MEASURE="VOBARSA"
FREQUENCY="Q" TIME_FORMAT="P3M" UNIT="EUR" POWERCODE="6"
REFERENCEPERIOD="2010">

<OECD:Obs TIME="2009-Q2" OBS_VALUE="288669.552976"/>
<OECD:Obs TIME="2009-Q3" OBS_VALUE="289372.504978"/>
<OECD:Obs TIME="2009-Q4" OBS_VALUE="292514.368989"/>
<OECD:Obs TIME="2010-Q1" OBS_VALUE="290540.292982"/>

</OECD:Series>
```


XBRL is the preferred language for regulatory reporting on statistical, regulatory and settlement reports, SDMX is mainly used by the OECD, IMF and the World Bank.[105]

[105] StatSilk (2021) n. pag.

3 Methodology

In the following chapter, the methodological approach, introduced at the beginning of this master's thesis, is examined in more detail. The selected methodological instruments are described and serve to substantiate the findings obtained from the literature in order to answer the formulated hypotheses and ultimately the research question. In the areas of finance, economics, business and technology, there are a variety of methods and techniques, which means that an appropriate methodology must be selected from among the quantitative or qualitative methods. Quantitative research typically involves the use of statistical or mathematical methods to analyse numerical data, while qualitative research focuses on analysing literature, interviews, or relationships without relying on numerical data. As this master's thesis is dedicated to the analysis of harmonised and integrated supervisory reporting frameworks and their impact on current practices in risk management, financial stability and compliance, qualitative research methods were chosen.[1]

3.1 Case Studies

A case study is an in-depth examination of a single case or a small number of cases within a real-world context, aiming to address specific research objectives or questions. These cases can encompass both quantitative and qualitative data, with

[1] Basias/Pollalis (2018) pp. 91–95.

Supplementary Information The online version contains supplementary material available at https://doi.org/10.1007/978-3-658-46447-9_3.

D. Dorrer, *Introduction of IReF*, BestMasters,
https://doi.org/10.1007/978-3-658-46447-9_3

the researcher choosing the most appropriate design for the study. They utilize a variety of research tools, including interviews, documentation analysis and direct observations, to gather relevant data.[2] Building on this foundation, case studies can be utilised to develop theoretical frameworks based on real-life examples. Subsequently, these findings can be further validated and enriched through qualitative or quantitative approaches.[3] In this master's thesis, real-life case studies as practical illustrations will be incorporated. These case studies will exemplify the application of the integrated reporting framework in real-world scenarios, offering valuable insights into its practical implementation and effectiveness for risk management practices, regulatory compliance and overall financial stability among various financial institutions operating in the Eurozone. Expert interviews will play a fundamental role in improving the depth of this master's thesis and will enable the integration of real-life insights and practical expertise into the research findings.

3.2 Expert Interviews

As part of qualitative research, expert interviews have proven to be reliable for gathering specific information. The fundamental concept of expert interviews is to obtain insights from individuals who have specialised knowledge in a particular area relevant to the researcher's interests. Experts are identified based on their roles in decision-making positions or their access to unique and relevant information.[4] The semi-structured interview style was chosen for this master's thesis. This approach offers flexibility while maintaining the necessary focus, as the questions can be adapted depending on the interview partner. The primary objective is to obtain an insight into the participants' perspective on the impact of harmonised and integrated supervisory reporting in the Eurozone, including various aspects related to risk management practices, regulatory compliance and financial stability. To facilitate the interviews, an interview guide is prepared in advance and made available to the experts. This guide serves as an orientation for the participants and helps them to prepare their answers to the questions. The questions are intentionally open-ended to encourage a wide range of insights and perspectives. Furthermore, in semi-structured interviews, the order of the questions can be adjusted depending on the course of the conversation, allowing for

[2] Mohajan (2018) pp. 32–33.

[3] Gustafsson (2017) pp. 5–6.

[4] Kleres (2015) pp. 90–91.

a dynamic exploration of the research topic.[5] For the interviews, a sample of five experts was selected. The emphasis was placed on experts with experience at both the Austrian National Bank and the European Central Bank, particularly those involved in projects related to integrating supervisory systems. Additionally, to capture insights into technological aspects, two experts from AuRep, an Austrian company specializing in supervisory reporting and collaborating with the OeNB, were interviewed.

3.2.1 Evaluation Method

In this master's thesis, qualitative content analysis was employed to address the research question. Qualitative content analysis provides a systematic approach to analysing textual data and enables the identification of patterns, themes and meanings in the interview transcripts. This methodological approach was chosen as it allows in-depth access to the participants' perspectives and experiences and is consistent with the qualitative nature of the research. The semi-structured interview style used in the interviews led to the creation of transcripts, the audio recordings were transcribed into a written text and edited for coherence.[6] To conduct such analysis, a categorization system was developed for organizing and analysing the interview transcripts.[7] In this master's thesis, the primary focus will be on a deductive analysis by summarizing the key points of the interviews and interpreting them to address the research question.[8] The categorisation system involves dividing the topics covered in the interview guide into different categories that facilitate the analysis process and provide a structured framework for interpreting the interview data. The following categories were formed:

- Regulatory reporting trends
- Integrated regulatory reporting systems
- IReF
- BIRD
- Basic Cube system
- Comparative analysis
- Future implications

---

[5] Adeoye-Olatunde/Olenik (2021) pp. 1360–1363.

[6] Mayring (2014) p. 43.

[7] Wildemuth/Zhang (2017) pp. 1–4.

[8] Mayring (2014) pp. 65–66.

Empirical Analysis 4

4.1 Integrated Supervisory Reporting

Data reporting and user requirements have expanded significantly and have become increasingly granular and complex, particularly in the area of statistics and central bank supervision. In the past, each country in the EU has developed its own methodology for data collection, which has led to redundant systems and a lack of data consistency. This fragmentation makes it difficult to gain a comprehensive understanding of the entire reporting and collection process.[1] To address this challenge, the ESCB considered the establishment of a common European information system. Against this backdrop, in 2013, the ESCB Statistics Committee formed the Groupe de Réflexion on the Integration of Statistical and Supervisory Data (GRISS). GRISS was tasked with adopting an integrated approach to managing data needs across various domains like monetary policy and supervision. This approach aimed to view data as part of a unified system, from collection to utilization. Essentially, the focus was on maximizing the use of existing data, so the multi-use of data, rather than generating new reports for each specific requirement. GRISS's efforts led to the consensus on eight actionable recommendations. The foremost among these was initiating the development of a comprehensive and standardized common reporting framework for banks to transmit data to European NCBs/NCAs. Consequently, in 2014, the Statistics Committee established the European Reporting Framework (ERF). The underlying concept of the ERF is to pursue an integrated and harmonised approach to

[1] Kienecker et al. (2018) pp. 22–25.

D. Dorrer, *Introduction of IReF*, BestMasters,
https://doi.org/10.1007/978-3-658-46447-9_4

collect a range of data required initially for various statistical purposes and subsequently for banking supervision. At present, this data is scattered across numerous individual reports. The aim is to create a "primary reporting framework" for the routine transmission of data from reporting agents to national central banks and other supervisory authorities. All the information needed for understanding the reporting requirements are described in the Single Data Dictionary (SDD).[2] EU banks are obligated to report a variety of data, however, only a few euro area countries have fully implemented integrated national collection frameworks. [3] In 2018, a significant rebranding occurred as the ERF transitioned into the Integrated Reporting Framework (IReF), reflecting a more cohesive and streamlined approach to reporting. Additionally, this renaming coincided with the integration of the Banks' Integrated Reporting Dictionary (BIRD), further enhancing the framework's efficiency and effectiveness in facilitating reporting processes.[4] As illustrated in Fig. 4.1 a problem related to non-harmonised reporting in the EU banking sector is the lack of consistency and compatibility among different reporting systems used by national central banks. Each national central bank may have its own reporting framework, which can lead to discrepancies in data collection methods, formats and standards. This lack of harmonisation makes it challenging to compare and aggregate data across different states, hindering the ability to conduct comprehensive analyses and assessments of the overall financial stability and risk within the EU banking system. Furthermore, it increases the burden on banks operating in multiple states, as they must navigate and comply with varying reporting requirements, potentially resulting in inefficiencies and increased compliance costs.[5]

[2] Turner/Sedlacek (2015) pp. 1–5.

[3] European Central Bank (2022) pp. 1–2.

[4] Kienecker et al. (2018) p. 38.

[5] European Central Bank (2022) pp. 2–8.

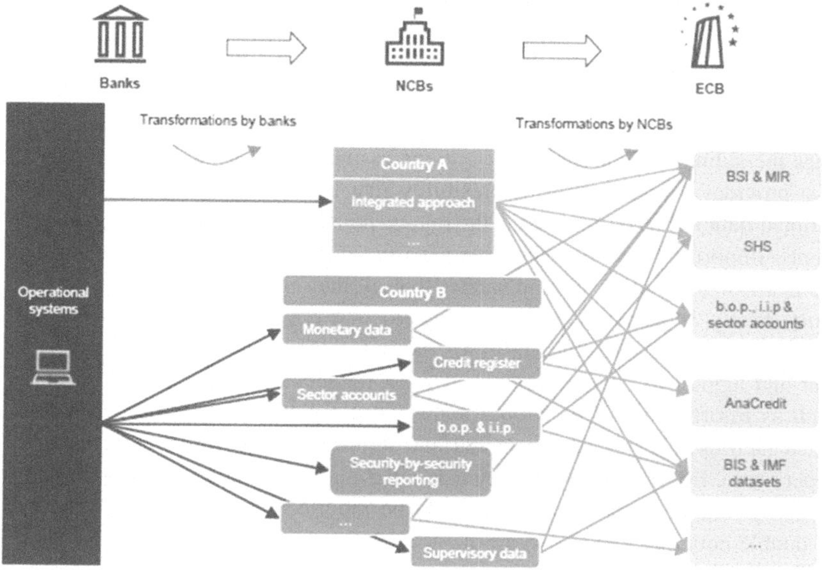

Fig. 4.1 Current data collecting approach[6]

An integrated reporting system offers a structured approach to the reporting process, that aims to improve the efficiency and effectiveness of data collection and analysis, thereby improving regulatory reporting. By harmonising reporting procedures and standards, an integrated system facilitates clearer communication and better alignment of regulatory objectives, ultimately contributing to a more resilient and transparent financial ecosystem. An integrated reporting system consolidates reporting processes into a unified ecosystem for both reporting institutions and authorities. Its framework operates on the principle of "define data once and report once," saving costs and boosting analytical capabilities. Moreover, it promotes information exchange among authorities, bolstering governance. By leveraging best practices in data management and technology, such a system enables a more streamlined and digitalized reporting process, enhancing efficiency and accuracy and consequently reducing the costs of supervisory reporting.[7]

---

[6] European Central Bank (2022) p. 2.

[7] European Central Bank (2022) pp. 2–8.

4.1.1 Central Data Collection Point

The challenge posed by non-integrated reporting, as illustrated in Fig. 4.1, requires the establishment of a central data collection point as a strategic solution. This central point serves as a central unified reporting entry point that streamlines the submission of statistical, settlement and regulatory data from banks. It also provides a crucial layer of flexibility that accommodates both ad hoc and national data requests, ensuring a flexible response to evolving reporting requirements. Importantly, adherence to a standardized data dictionary and model is at the heart of this initiative. It mandates that all data transfers to the central body must strictly adhere to a common standard that covers a comprehensive range of datasets. In addition, the ability of the hub to seamlessly process both granular and aggregated data is critical. It must be able to process complex details, such as information on individual loans for statistical analysis, but also aggregated metrics, like regulatory capital and liquidity ratios, which are critical for supervision. Ensuring data integrity is another important aspect of the central collection point. Each data point may only be reported once to minimize the risk of double counting and to ensure the accuracy and reliability of the information collected. Finally, by facilitating access for European and national authorities, the central collection point serves as a hub for transparency and cooperation. Authorized bodies, including the ECB, SRB, EBA, NCBs, NRAs and NCAs, can quickly access relevant data, enabling informed decision-making and regulatory oversight. The new integrated IReF system is designed to fulfil these requirements of a central data collection point.[8]

4.1.2 Standard Data Dictionary

The creation of and adherence to a standardized data dictionary is fundamental to the functioning of an integrated reporting system and is one of its most important foundations. This standardized repository includes definitions for all concepts provided for the various European and national reporting regulations.[9] A comprehensive data dictionary goes beyond mere definitions and includes additional components, such as transformation rules, validation criteria for the final output data and the underlying data model representation such as the EBA data point model or the SMCube information model. These transformation rules clarify the

[8] European Central Bank (2020) pp. 15–18.

[9] European Banking Authority (2021) p. 24.

relationships between the concepts of the dictionary or describe the necessary steps to derive higher-level concepts from more granular data elements within the dictionary. Moreover, a single data dictionary can achieve reporting integration and methodological and semantic integration. Reporting integration aims to collect data only once, at a level of granularity, suitable for different reporting requirements. In addition, methodological and semantic Integration aims to establish uniformity in syntax, concepts and definitions across diverse surveys and domains. The Euro system has initiated efforts towards the development of the Single Data Dictionary and the Banks' Integrated Reporting Dictionary. The BIRD consolidates the definitions of prudential, statistical, resolution and reporting requirements mandated by various EU laws. Additionally, it encompasses transformation rules designed to derive these data from banks' internal systems. This initiative appears to be a promising step towards the realization of a comprehensive data dictionary spanning resolution, statistical and prudential reporting domains.[10]

4.1.3 SDD

The Single Data Dictionary initiative led by the ECB is an important step towards the standardization of metadata for datasets used within the ECB and across the ESCB. Currently, different reporting regulations use various terminology or coding schemes to describe similar concepts. The main objective of the SDD initiative is to change the reporting and analysis of data by establishing clear and common definitions for the data provided or developed by the ECB. This standardization enables more comprehensive and accurate analyses by ensuring that datasets are described according to a common standard. Furthermore, the benefits of the SDD initiative extend not only to the ECB and its stakeholders, but also to the financial sector. The ESCB and financial institutions utilize the SDD in various data collection processes, e.g. via the BIRD. Fig. 4.2 likely illustrates how integrating reporting requirements with the SDD can help reduce redundancies by standardizing codes for the same meaning across different reporting frameworks or requirements.[11]

---

[10] European Central Bank (2020) pp. 11–12.

[11] Israël (2018) pp. 3–5.

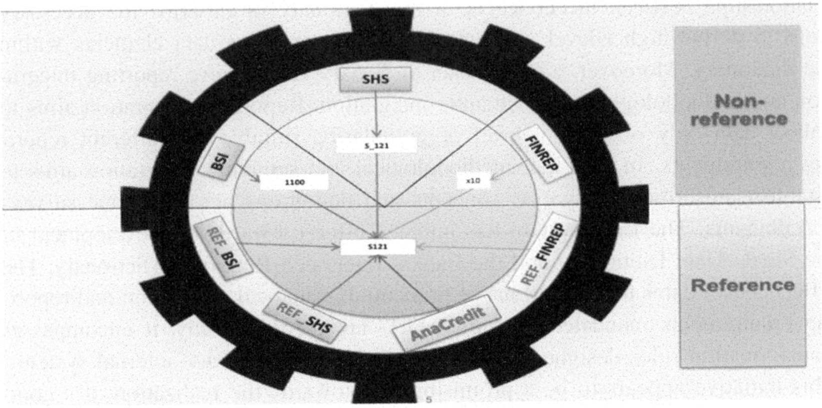

Fig. 4.2 Example of semantic integration[12]

4.1.4 Example of the Reporting Burden

The lack of harmonisation leads to data redundancies and increased workload for employees, which in turn leads to higher costs for the banks. Fig. 4.3 clearly illustrates the reporting burden under the current regulatory system for an Austrian bank. Currently, a bank has to report similar or overlapping data five different times for a loan. This challenge increases dramatically for cross-border activities, as different semantics and other problems lead to even more data redundancies.[13]

---

[12] Israël (2018) p. 5.

[13] Turner/Sedlacek (2015) pp. 1–3.

Reporting requirement	Template	Value
FinRep solo[2] (as of June 2016)	Templ. 1.1 (Non-trading debt instruments measured at a cost-based method - sum)	(Net) carrying amounts (incl. accrued interest)
	Templ. 4.9 (Breakdown by counterparty sector and impairment status)	(Gross) carrying amounts and allowances
	Templ. 5 (Breakdown by product, collaterals, subordination each with economic sector)	(Net) carrying amounts
	Templ. 6 (Breakdown by industry classification and performing status)	(Gross) carrying amounts
	Templ. 9.1 (Loan commitments by performing status)	Nominal amounts
	Templ. 18 (Breakdown by economic sector and performing/non-performing categories)	(Gross) carrying amounts, allowances
	Templ. 19 (Information on forborne exposures by economic sector and performing status)	(Gross) carrying amounts, allowances
	Templ. 20.4 (Breakdown by residence of the counterparty, economic sector and forbearance respectively performing status)	(Gross) carrying amounts, allowances
National Financial Market Stability Reports	Breakdown by remaining maturity and counterparty sector	(Net) carrying amounts
	Breakdown by currency, economic sector and redemption details	(Net) carrying amounts
ECB – MFI Balance Sheet Items (BSI)	Breakdown by original maturity, economic sector and residence of the counterparty	(Gross) carrying amounts (excl. accrued interest)
	Breakdown by product type and residence of the counterparty	(Gross) carrying amounts
	Breakdown by currency, economic sector and residence of the counterparty	(Gross) carrying amounts
	Loan transfers broken down by counterparty of the transfer and economic sector of the borrower	Net flows
	Breakdown by industrial classification	(Gross) carrying amounts
BoP & IIP[3]	Cross boarder loans by original maturity, economic sector and residence of the counterparty	(Gross) carrying amounts, transactions
National Central Credit Register (CCR)	Breakdown by borrower, product type, collateral type	(Gross) carrying amounts, credit lines, allowances

Fig. 4.3 Data redundancies for reporting a loan[14]

[14] Turner/Sedlacek (2015) p. 2.

4.2 Basic Cube of the Austrian National Bank

The Integrated Reporting Data Model, or the "Basic Cube," serves as a foundational reporting tool for the Austrian National Bank (OeNB) and was one of the first attempts to establish a harmonised reporting system in the Eurozone. Its underlying technology connects data points associated with specific business cases and their corresponding attributes. Its purpose is to construct a multidimensional data matrix, facilitating a comprehensive representation of various aspects of reporting requirements. The main objective is to empower banks to prepare and submit any legally mandated report, whether dictated by the Austrian Banking Act, the Foreign Exchange Act, ECB regulations, EBA Implementing Technical Standards, or others, in a uniform and consistent manner, leaving no room for interpretation. By leveraging this data cube, banks can ensure consistency across their reporting processes, streamlining compliance efforts and enhancing regulatory adherence.[15] The current supervisory reporting standards require the collection of multiple data in several reports, the provided templates, such as for FINREP or COREP reports, are therefore not free of redundancy. The Austrian Basic Cube tries to collect supervisory and monetary data within a limited amount of so-called smart cubes.[16]

Technically, smart cubes are multidimensional data models, structured for national and international reporting obligations. Reporting banks generate smart cubes through the application of specialized aggregation and selection algorithms to the dataset contained within their respective Basic Cubes.[17] Smart cubes are used to generate various secondary statistics. Supervisory reporting requirements are collected in the form of data templates. The key concept of the Basic Cube reporting data model is to use a single data source, such as a template to create all reporting frameworks. As illustrated in Fig. 4.4, granular data are sourced directly from banks' core systems and aggregated into the Basic Cube. This cube serves as the foundation for meeting reporting requirements, whether through the creation of smart cubes or supervisory reporting templates. To ensure consistency and compliance, harmonised enrichment algorithms and transformation rules are applied to the data within the Basic Cube. These processes enhance the data's quality and relevance, aligning it with regulatory standards and facilitating accurate reporting.[18]

---

[15] Oesterreichische Nationalbank (n.d.d) n.pag.

[16] Hille (2013) pp. 271–273.

[17] Hille (2013) pp. 271–273.

[18] Kienecker et al. (2018) pp. 27–29.

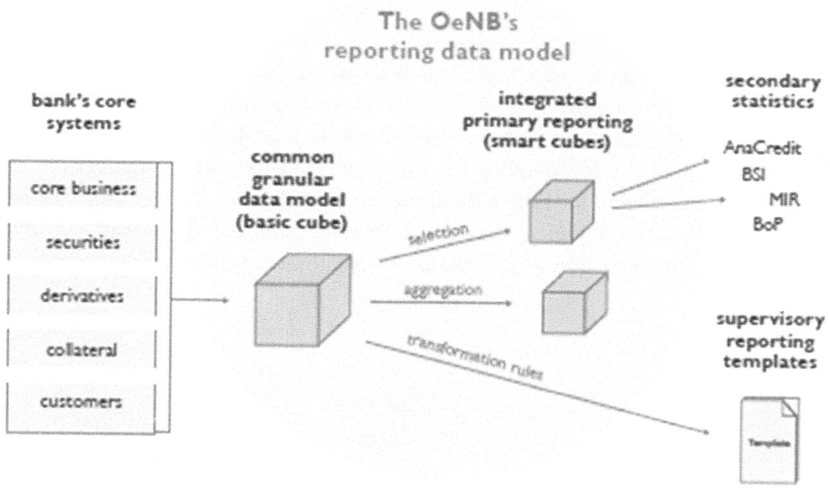

Fig. 4.4 Data flow in the OeNB data model[19]

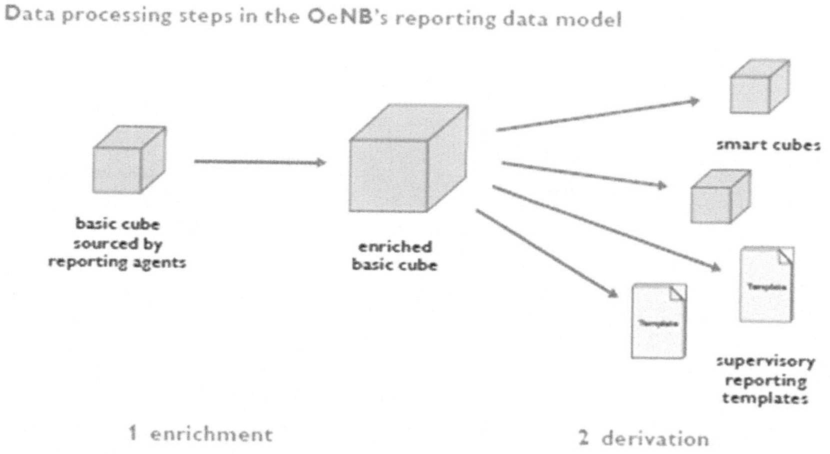

Fig. 4.5 Data processing in the Austrian model[20]

[19] Kienecker et al. (2018) p. 27.
[20] Kienecker et al. (2018) p. 30.

As seen in Fig. 4.5, the Basic Cube distinguishes between the smart cubes and the supervisory reporting templates. The OeNB's reporting model ensures data consistency across frameworks through a single, granular database, benefiting users and reporting agents with higher quality data and reduced revisions. Integration minimises reporting frameworks, cutting costs and enabling OeNB to handle aggregation. However, it increases content complexity, requiring advanced quality checks and technical understanding for ERM and transformation languages.[21]

For the Basic Cube, an Entity-Relationship model was used, as they can be easily converted into a logical database structure. This has the advantage that it can be implemented into any database management system of a commercial bank.[22]

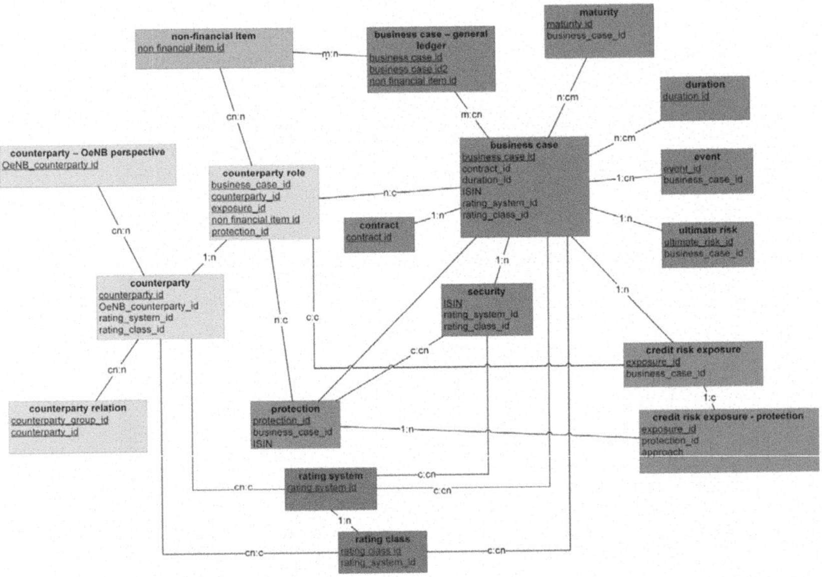

Fig. 4.6 ERD of the Basic Cube[23]

[21] Kienecker et al. (2018) pp. 34–35.

[22] Hille (2013) p. 272.

[23] Kienecker et al. (2018) p. 28.

In the Basic Cube, various entities are present, each represented as a box within the ERM model, encompassing different types of information. Every financial instrument held by the reporting agent, whether it's a loan, deposit, security, or derivative, finds representation within the business case entity of the Basic Cube model as seen in Fig. 4.6. Numerous attributes are accessible at the instrument level, detailing all relevant characteristics of a business case necessary to fulfil different reporting requirements. These attributes may include information, such as the type of instrument, issue and maturity dates, purpose of a loan and accounting classification. Furthermore, most attributes come with a predefined code set, offering a level of granularity sufficient to address all reporting requirements integrated into the OeNB's reporting data model. This structured approach ensures consistency and comprehensiveness in reporting while, meeting the varied needs of regulatory compliance.[24] Austrian banks use a special software to provide microdata on individual transactions, such as loans. This data is stored in the Basic Cubes, which are defined according to a standardized data model defined by the OeNB and the banks. The Basic Cubes are supplemented by additional attributes and the required reports are derived from them by generating multidimensional data cubes, the smart cubes. These smart cubes are then delivered to the OeNB and analysed there. In the end, the reported data is sent via the XBRL to the EBA or to the BIS. This concept for the transmission of statistical data increases the delivery of data and makes redundant data deliveries obsolete. Consequently, reported data can be used to create various regulatory statistics.[25] The Basic Cube model from the OeNB serves as a blueprint for further integrated reporting projects like the BIRD or the IReF (Fig. 4.7).

---

[24] Kienecker et al. (2018) pp. 28–29.

[25] Lux/Piechocki (2015) pp. 661–663.

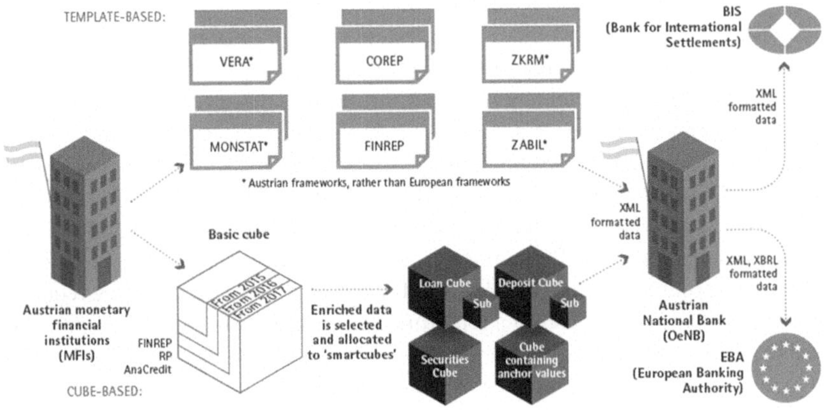

Fig. 4.7 Austrian reporting system[26]

4.2.1 Examples of Reporting

4.2.2 Financial Guarantee[27]

The reporter is an Austrian financial institution (Identification Number 00000004). The reporter issues a financial guarantee (ID Instr_Guarantee1) for a domestic company (Identification Number 00000002). The beneficiary is an Austrian financial institution (Identification Number 00000001). The guarantee is for EUR 50,000,000. The contract was concluded on May 20, 2019 (Fig. 4.8).

[26] Lux/Piechocki (2015) p. 662.

[27] Oesterreichische Nationalbank (n. d. b) n.pag.

02. Nicht-verbriefte Anteilsrechte, außerbilanzielle Geschäfte (gem. CRR, Anhang I, exkl. Kreditzusagen) und regulatorische Netting-Sätze

02.02. Instrument-Daten

Attribut	Code	Nicht-verbriefte Anteilsrechte, außerbilanzielle Geschäfte (gem. CRR, Anhang I, exkl. Kreditzusagen) und Regulatorische Netting-Sätze – Rechtsträger iSd Art. 1(5) der AnaCredit-VO über 25.000 – Granularität: Instrument
SC_Mandant_Identnummer	INMAN	00000004
SC_Instrument_ID	INSID	Instr_Garantie1
SC_Rechtstraeger_Kennzeichen	JUPKZ	J (Ja)
SC_Art_des_Instruments_Code	INTAC	FG (Finanzgarantien (exklusive Kreditderivate)
SC_Schuldnergruppe_Kennzeichen	SGRKZ	N (Nein)

02.03. Finanzdaten

Attribut	Code	Nicht-verbriefte Anteilsrechte, außerbilanzielle Geschäfte (gem. CRR, Anhang I, exkl. Kreditzusagen) und Regulatorische Netting-Sätze – Rechtsträger iSd Art. 1(5) der AnaCredit-VO über 25.000 – Granularität: Instrument
SC_Mandant_Identnummer	INMAN	00000004
SC_Instrument_ID	INSID	Instr_Garantie1
SC_Ratingsystem_intern	RASYI	-
SC_Bonitaetsklasse_intern	BOSYI	-
Buchwert	BW	-
Nominale	NN	50 000 000
nicht-ausgenützter Rahmen	NAR	0
Ausfallwahrscheinlichkeit	PD	-

02.04. Daten zu Vertragspartner-Instrument

Attribut	Code	Nicht-verbriefte Anteilsrechte, außerbilanzielle Geschäfte (gem. CRR, Anhang I, exkl. Kreditzusagen) und Regulatorische Netting-Sätze – Rechtsträger iSd Art. 1(5) der AnaCredit-VO über 25.000 – Granularität: Instrument	Nicht-verbriefte Anteilsrechte, außerbilanzielle Geschäfte (gem. CRR, Anhang I, exkl. Kreditzusagen) und Regulatorische Netting-Sätze – Rechtsträger iSd Art. 1(5) der AnaCredit-VO über 25.000 – Granularität: Instrument
SC_Mandant_Identnummer	INMAN	00000004	00000004
SC_Vertragspartner_Identnummer	INVEP	00000001	00000002
SC_Instrument_ID	INSID	Instr_Garantie1	Instr_Garantie1
SC_Rolle_Code	ROLEC	BG (Begünstigter)	KN (Kreditnehmer lt. GKE)

Fig. 4.8 Representation of the template[28]

[28] Oesterreichische Nationalbank (n. d. b) n.pag.

Firstly, the bank responsible for arranging the guarantee is mandated to report to the OeNB. It is required to fill out the templates within the Basic Cube framework. Within the initial spreadsheet labeled 02.02. "Instrument-Daten," general instrument data is entered. Each attribute is designated by a specific code; for instance, SC_Instrument_ID is represented by INSID. General instrument data encompasses details, such as the issued guarantee of reporter 00000004. Subsequently, in the 02.03. "Finanzdaten" sheet, details regarding the guarantee, such as the amount of EUR 50,000,000, are provided. Finally, the 02.04. "Daten zu Vertragspartner-Instrument" sheet contains information on the contract partners, including the beneficiary of the guarantee and the borrower (Fig. 4.9).

02. Nicht-verbriefte Anteilsrechte, außerbilanzielle Geschäfte (gem. CRR, Anhang I, exkl. Kreditzusagen) und regulatorische Netting-Sätze

02. 10. Kreditrisikodaten

		Nicht-verbriefte Anteilsrechte, außerbilanzielle Geschäfte (gem. CRR, Anhang I, exkl. Kreditzusagen) und Regulatorische Netting-Sätze
		Rechtsträger iSd Art. 1(5) der AnaCredit-VO über 25.000
Attribut	Code	Granularität: Exposure
SC_Mandant_Identnummer	INMAN	00000004
SC_Exposure_ID	EXPID	Exposure_Garantie1
SC_Instrument_ID	INSID	Instr_Garantie1
SC_Ansatz_zur_Berechnung_des_Kapitals_fuer_Aufsichtszwecke_Code	AEMBC	S (Standardansatz)
SC_Risikopositionsklasse_Code	FK	S0700 (gegenüber Unternehmen)
SC_Forderungskategorie_Code	FOKAC	OFFB (Offbalance)
SC_Berechnungsmethode_Gegenparteiausfallsrisiko_Code	BMGAC	-
SC_Vertragspartner_Identnummer	INVEP	00000002
Risikopositionswert	RP	50 000 000
Erwarteter Verlust	EL	-
Risikogewichteter Positionsbetrag nach Anwendung des KMU-Faktors	RWA	10 000 000

Fig. 4.9 Credit risk data source[29]

Following this, in the 02.10. "Kreditrisikodaten" template, which translates to credit risk data, reporting obligations must be fulfilled. Here, the attribute for calculating own funds requirements must be specified, denoted as "S" for the standard approach under the CRR. Subsequently, a figure of EUR 10,000,000 is determined using the standard approach. Additional requirements in this table comprise the risk amount and the contract partner 00000002 (Fig. 4.10).

[29] Oesterreichische Nationalbank (n. d. b) n.pag.

04. Vertragspartner und Exposure-zugeordnete Einheiten

04.09. Daten zu Vertragspartnern und Exposure-zugeordnete Einheiten

		Einzelschuldner	Einzelschuldner
		Rechtsträger iSd Art. 1(5) der AnaCredit-VO über 25.000 bzw. natürliche Person über 350.000	Rechtsträger iSd Art. 1(5) der AnaCredit-VO über 25.000 bzw. natürliche Person über 350.000
Attribut	Code	Granularität: Schuldner	Granularität: Schuldner
SC_Vertragspartner_Identnummer	INVEP	00000001	00000002
SC_Ausfallstatus_Datum	AFSTD		-
SC_Ratingsystem_intern	RASYI		Ratingsystem_Unternehmen
SC_Bonitaetsklasse_intern	BOSYI		AAA
SC_Ratingsystem_standardisiert_Code	RASYS		00069
SC_Bonitaetsklasse_standardisiert_Code	BOSYS		Aaa
Ausfallwahrscheinlichkeit	PD		0,02%

Fig. 4.10 Details regarding contract partners[30]

The subsequent template, 04.09. "Daten zu Vertragspartnern und Exposure—zugeordnete Einheiten," provides insights into the contract partners and their associated ratings. The company holds a credit rating of AAA with a PD of 0.02%. The rating was assigned using "O0069", indicating a Moody's rating.

Finally, the "06. Meldung der institutsinternen Ratingsysteme" template requests data regarding the internal rating system (Fig. 4.11).

Algorithms play a crucial role in the pre-processing of data in the OeNB's Basic Cube and enable the immediate identification and elimination of incorrect data. This process significantly improves the quality and processing speed of the reported data. Among the various algorithms used, the XEN algorithm will be provided as an example.

[30] Oesterreichische Nationalbank (n. d. b) n.pag.

06. Meldung der institutsinternen Ratingsysteme

06.13. Auflistung der Ratingsysteme

Attribut	Code	geratete Kreditnehmer, Exposure-zugeordnete Einheiten und Instrumente Granularität: Ratingsystem
SC_Ratingsystem_intern	RASYI	**Ratingsystem_Unternehmen**
SC_Ratingsystem_Quelle_Identnummer	RAQID	-
SC_Abgenommenes_IRB_Ratingsystem_Kennzeichen	AIRKZ	**N (Nein)**
SC_Verwendung_fuer_Credit_Claims_Kennzeichen	VCCKZ	**N (Nein)**
Bezeichnung Ratingsystem	RSB	**Ratingsystem für in AT ansässige Unternehmen mit Bilanzsumme > 100 Mio.**

06.14. Bonitätsklassen je Ratingsystem

Attribut	Code	geratete Kreditnehmer, Exposure-zugeordnete Einheiten und Instrumente Granularität: Bonitätsklasse
SC_Bonitaetsklasse_intern	BOSYI	~~Ratingsystem_Unternehmen~~
SC_Ratingsystem_intern	RASYI	~~AAA~~
Beschreibung Bonitätsklasse	BKB	
PD-Untergrenze	PDU	
PD-Obergrenze	PDO	

Fig. 4.11 Reporting of rating systems[31]

4.2.3 XEN Algorithms

By using so-called XEN algorithms, also referred to as transformation rules for the enrichment of data, the reported data can be pre-processed to avoid redundancies. In the given example, the algorithm, XEN_Nominal, is aimed at calculating the total nominal value of mortgages associated with a security, specifically focusing on real estate securities. The algorithm iterates over all mortgages related to the security, specifically targeting real estate securities. In this scenario, it calculates the sum of the nominal values of these mortgages.[32]

[31] Oesterreichische Nationalbank (n. d. b) n.pag.

[32] Oesterreichische Nationalbank (n.d.a) n.pag.

FUNCTION

XEN_Nominal *(ST.AI_Mandant MA, ST.AI_Stichtag_Datum repDate, ST.AI_Sicherheiten_ID sichId)*

//(I) Identifikation von Input-Parametern

sicherheitentyp= SELEKTIERE ST.ST03_Sicherheitenkategorie_Code VON ST_Sicherheiten_Stammdaten

hypotheken_ids= SELEKTIERE ALLE HY.AI_Hypothek_ID VON HY_Hypothek VON ST_Sicherheiten_Stammdaten

//(II) Verarbeitung der Parameter

WENN (sicherheitentyp ENTHAELT ("Wohnimmobilie (WI)", "Anrechnungsfähige Gewerbeimmobilien (GB)", "Sonstige Gewerbeimmobilien (SI)")

rValue = 0

ITERIERE hypothek VON (0, Max(hypotheken_ids))

nn = SELEKTIERE HYW.Wert VON HYW_Hypothek_Wert MIT HYW.AI_Wertart_Code ISTGLEICH "Nominale (NN)" UND HYW.AI_Hypothek_ID ISTGLEICH hypothek

rValue = rValue +nn

ITERATION ENDE

ENDE

//(III) Rückgabe

RUECKGABE rValue

FUNKTIONSENDE

4.3 BIRD

As new statistical, regulatory or resolution frameworks emerge or existing ones are updated, banks currently have to interpret the reporting requirements independently and work out for themselves what they need to report, frequently leading to problems. The Banks' Integrated Reporting Dictionary simplifies this process by providing an integrated, comprehensive and redundancy-free data model. BIRD is a documentation of reporting content that aims to support the banking industry in structuring its reporting-relevant data and to minimize burdens arising from regulations. It combines definitions of the prudential, statistical and resolution data to be reported. Based on the GRISS report in 2015, the Statistics Committee of the European System of Central Banks embarked on a BIRD pilot initiative targeting two specific statistical areas proposed following an ECB workshop with the banking sector namely AnaCredit and SHS. Building upon the pilot's success, in June 2018, the EBA's ITS for FINREP were integrated into BIRD. Subsequently, the scope of application will be extended to other supervisory requirements, including COREP, BSI, MIR and Asset Encumbrance.[33]

The goal of the BIRD initiative is to create an input data model at the European level, as well as a harmonised data dictionary. This model is designed to harmonise and integrate banks' internal reporting processes, aligning them with a standardized framework like the Basic Cube and transformation rules found in the OeNB's reporting data model. By establishing consistency and integration in reporting to regulatory authorities, BIRD aims to enhance comparability and efficiency across the banking sector.[34]

Through BIRD, concepts are identified and described only once, making it easier for banks to decide which data sources to use and exactly how to process them. It is important to recognize that BIRD acts as a reference tool and not as an IT solution. It does not change the banks' internal IT systems, nor does it involve mapping data from these systems to BIRD components, such as the logical data model or the input layer. Furthermore, BIRD is not a regulatory mandate and does not introduce any new requirements. BIRD typically includes definitions, classifications and instructions for reporting various financial elements, such as assets, liabilities, income, expenses and capital. By following the guidelines outlined in BIRD, banks can streamline their reporting processes, improve data quality and facilitate better decision-making by stakeholders.[35]

4.3.1 Methodology

The BIRD has translated the DPM into the SMCube format. In particular, the content of the EBA DPM has been automatically imported into the SMCube methodology from the XBRL taxonomies.[36] The BIRD documentation is based on the so-called input approach. Based on the reporting-relevant content, which is defined as closely as possible to the banks' systems, the so-called input layer,

---

[33] European Central Bank (n.d.g) n.pag.

[34] Kienecker et al. (2018) p. 37.

[35] European Central Bank (n.d.g) n.pag.

[36] European Central Bank (2019) pp. 64–68.

transformation rules are used to describe how the reports can be derived to generate the required reports. The input layer of the BIRD corresponds to the Basic Cube in the Austrian data model (Fig. 4.12).[37]

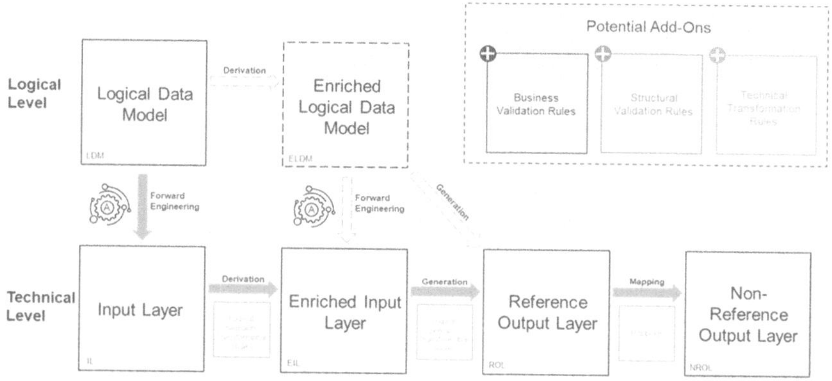

Fig. 4.12 Methodology of BIRD[38]

The BIRD methodology encompasses two key elements, such as the BIRD process and the BIRD components. The BIRD process outlines the end-to-end workflow, detailing how BIRD is designed to operate efficiently. The BIRD components include data structures and connecting elements essential for BIRD's functionality. The BIRD process portrays the workflow from input to output. In this process, data structure components, depicted as blue boxes, interconnect via connecting components, represented by yellow arrows. These data structure components, called layers, such as the Logical Data Model and the Input Layer, illustrate the sequential stages from input to output. The connecting components encompass forward engineering, logical/semantic transformation rules and mappings. These elements establish the procedures facilitating the connection of elements across BIRD layers throughout the entire process. Additionally, validation components comprise business and structural validation rules, ensuring data consistency, integrity and quality. These rules are devised for BIRD layers when resources permit. The BIRD process is divided into two levels: the logical level and the physical level. Connecting components not only link BIRD layers within

[37] Kienecker et al. (2018) pp. 37–38.

[38] European Central Bank (n.d.g) n.pag.

each level but also establish a bridge between the two levels through forward engineering.[39]

The logical level consists of the BIRD's logical data model (LDM) and the Enriched Logical Data Model (ELDM). The logical level focuses on the conceptual and business aspects of the system. The data models are normalized entity-relationship models. In this structure, they take the form of database entities organized into tables, with attributes described and connected through multiple relations based on predefined normalization principles.[40] The LDM describes the business requirements and their interrelationships and helps users to understand them for reporting purposes. Its harmonised definitions provide a solid mathematical basis for the consistent development of other BIRD layers. The ELDM contains all attributes from the derivation transformation rules. For example, it contains attributes, such as company size or annual turnover, which are derived from variables in the LDM.[41]

The technical level consists of Input Layer (IL), the Enriched Input Layer (EIL), the Reference Output Layer (ROL) and the Non-Reference Output Layer (NROL). The technical level deals with the implementation details. It involves translating the conceptual design from the logical level into specific technologies, platforms and programming languages. The BIRD layers represent the structural elements of data that outline the progression from input to output. These layers are constructed utilizing the principles of the SMCube methodology. IL and EIL also represent entity-relationship models.[42]

The BIRD IL serves as a blueprint for a physical interface model and is derived from the BIRD LDM through forward engineering. Although it comprises the same business components as the LDM, it is leaner and more user-friendly and omits some structural features. The IL can serve as a starting point for the technical implementation, e.g. in a database setup. The EIL is an extension of the BIRD IL and contains all attributes that are derived from the derivation transformation rules. It is a further development of the ELDM. Both the ROL and the NROL serve to describe reporting data, such as AnaCredit. However, while the ROL employs reference codes derived from the BIRD lexicon to delineate regulatory reporting requirements, the NROL utilizes non-reference codes sourced from the EBA Data Point Model for the same purpose. Unlike other BIRD layers,

---

[39] European Central Bank (n.d.g) n.pag.

[40] Bulut et al. (2022) p. 5.

[41] European Central Bank (n.d.g) n.pag.

[42] Bulut et al. (2022) p. 5.

the NROL adapts concepts and codes according to specific regulatory reporting needs, ensuring flexibility. Multiple NROLs are derived from a single ROL, ensuring semantic integration across BIRD layers. Connection components play a crucial role in establishing links between these layers by employing logical and semantic transformation rules, as well as mappings, also referred to as "forward engineering".[43]

Additionally, various validation components, including business and structural validation rules, are in place to uphold data consistency, integrity and quality. The logical structure of BIRD, LDM embeds dependencies that indirectly reflect validation rules. Additional validation rules, such as structural and business validation rules, can be introduced to improve consistency, integrity and data quality. Structural validation rules, which are crucial for ensuring the consistency of simplified layers, such as IL/EIL are automatically generated from the LDM during forward engineering. The validation rules are provided in a JSON format, so that they can be tested by users and receive feedback to further refine their content and format.[44] The physical model is derived from the logical model through a process known as forward engineering, where the logical design is transformed into a physical database schema tailored to the requirements of the target DBMS.

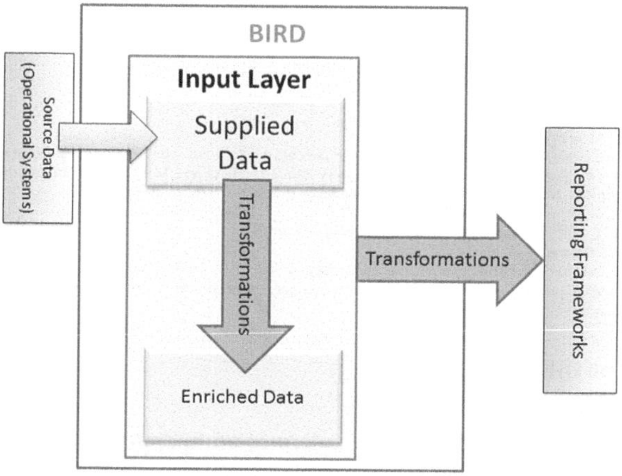

Fig. 4.13 BIRD's Input Layer[45]

---

[43] Bulut et al. (2022) pp. 5–7.

[44] European Central Bank (n.d.g) n.pag.

[45] Oesterreichische Nationalbank (n.d.c) n.pag.

As illustrated in Fig. 4.13, the source data from banks is sent to the input layer of the BIRD, where the data is transformed into enriched data and then ultimately sent to the reporting frameworks, also called output layer. This process involves the SMCube technology. Transformation rules are applied to create consistent and harmonised data. For the BIRD, the Validation and Transformation Language (VTL) was chosen to write the transformation rules.[46]

4.3.2 Example of a VTL Transformation Rule

```
define operator D_CRRYNG_AMNT (ACCNTNG_CLSSFCTN component, FV component, GRSS_CRRYNG_AMNT_E_INTRST
component,
                  ACCRD_INTRST component, FV_CHNG_HDG_ACCNTNG component, ACCMLTD_IMPRMNT component,
                  CRRYNG_AMNT component, IS_CRRYNG_AMNT_DRVD component)
  returns component is
    if IS_CRRYNG_AMNT_DRVD = "T"
    then
      if ACCNTNG_CLSSFCTN in {"14", "6", "8", "4", "2", "41"}
      then
        FV
      else
        GRSS_CRRYNG_AMNT_E_INTRST + ACCRD_INTRST - FV_CHNG_HDG_ACCNTNG - ACCMLTD_IMPRMNT
    else
      CRRYNG_AMNT
end operator;
```

Meanings of variables and codes used:
CRRYNG_AMNT: Carrying amount
ACCNTNG_CLSSFCTN: Accounting Classification (
2 = Financial assets held for trading; 6 = Financial assets at amortised cost; 8 = Financial assets at fair value through other comprehensive income; 4 = Financial assets designated at fair value through profit or loss; 14 = Cash balances at central banks and other demand deposits; 41 = Non-trading financial assets mandatorily at fair value through profit or loss)
FV: Fair value
GRSS_CRRYNG_AMNT_E_INTRST: Gross carrying amount excluding interest
ACCRD_INTRST: Accrued Interest
FV_CHNG_HDG_ACCNTNG: Fair value changes due to hedge accounting
IS_CRRYNG_AMNT_DRVD: Is carrying amount derived (parameter to trigger the generation of the Carrying amount)
ACCMLTD_IMPRMNT: Accumulated impairment

Fig. 4.14 VTL in BIRD[47]

The provided code, written in VTL, defines an operator named D_CRRYNG_AMNT. This operator calculates the carrying amount based on specified parameters. It first checks if the carrying amount is derived and evaluates the accounting classification. If the classification matches certain values, the carrying amount is

[46] Arru/Oddone (2022) pp. 4–6.

[47] Arru/Oddone (2022) p. 6.

set equal to the fair value (FV). Otherwise, it computes the carrying amount by subtracting fair value changes due to hedge accounting and accumulated impairment from the sum of gross carrying amount, excluding interest and accrued interest. If the carrying amount is not derived, it defaults to the parameter CRRYNG_AMNT. This approach ensures consistency and harmonisation in financial supervisory reporting (Fig. 4.14).

4.3.3 SMCube

The Single Multidimensional Metadata Model (SMCube), developed by the European Central Bank for the SDD and BIRD, serves as an information model for the abstract definition of dataset structures and associated features, such as exchange and transformations. Cubes in a database utilize tables to represent data. It is the methodology which serves as the basis for the BIRD metadata. This model goes beyond various existing methods, such as the DPM/XBRL and offers a higher level of abstraction to improve data integration.[48] Semantic integration ensures that all concepts used to describe statistical and supervisory data are encoded in a single and unambiguous manner. To achieve this, a mapping process has been implemented. The SMCube methodology offers a model capable of handling complex mappings (Fig. 4.15).[49]

[48] European Central Bank (2017) p. 3.

[49] European Central Bank (2019) pp. 64–68.

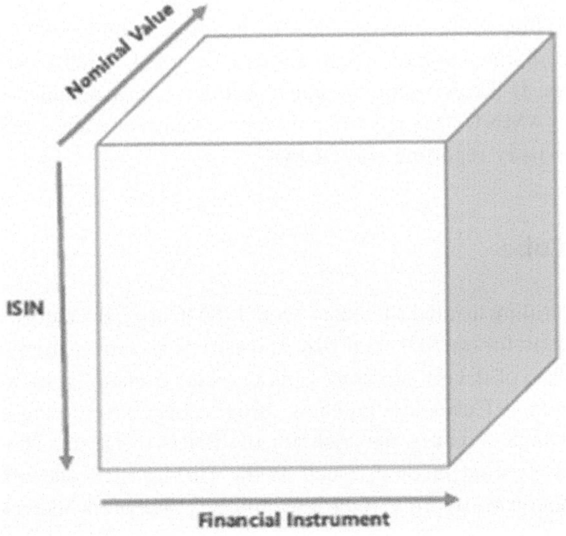

Fig. 4.15 SMCube[50]

Every layer of the BIRD is constructed using the SMCube Information Model. This implies that data is organized into tables resembling multidimensional cubes, comprised of rows and columns. Notably, the SMCube allows for the incorporation of more than three dimensions, enabling complex data structuring beyond traditional models.[51]

In Fig. 4.16, a financial institution uses the SMCube methodology and wants to enter some data about a security in a table for the collateral of a financial instrument. Following the SMCube methodology, the columns of the tables are referred to as variables and their definitions are independent of any specific cube. This approach offers the advantage of defining variables once and potentially utilizing them across multiple cubes. Each variable is associated with a domain that outlines the possible values for that variable. Domains can either be enumerations, containing a list of allowable values, or non-enumerations, characterized by a specific data type. Examples of non-enumerations include "ISIN" (String Domain), "Contract Start Date" (Date Domain), or "Fair Value"

[50] Bulut et al. (2022) p. 7.

[51] Bulut et al. (2022) p. 7.

(Monetary Domain). BIRD aims to simplify by harmonising statistical and supervisory needs. Banks often deal with the complexity of meeting diverse reporting demands for each regulatory requirement, resulting in repetitive data submissions (Fig. 4.17).[52]

SMCUBE
SECURITIES DATASET

ISIN	Type of instrument	Financial instrument	Inception Date	Legal final maturity date	Sub-ordinated debt	Nominal value	Fair Value	Accrued interest	Currency
YY3365923418	E_12	F_22	14/02/2018	14/06/2038	1	1000	1020	10	EUR
ZZ3441829454	E_11	F_211	05/11/2016			10000	10050		USD

Fig. 4.16 Example SMCube methodology[53]

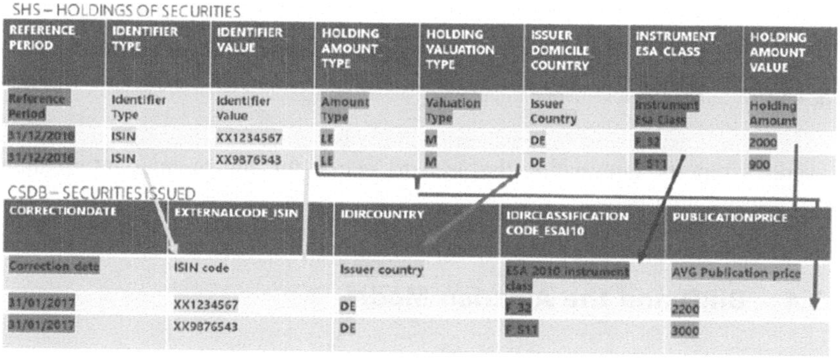

Fig. 4.17 Example without semantic integration[54]

The reports have varying column names and formats. For instance, the SHS report necessitates two columns for ISIN, while the CSDB report uses only one. This inconsistency creates redundancy and increases time spent on data entry. The upcoming figure depicts how banks could handle processed financial data records in the context of BIRD and the underlying SMCube methodology. By

[52] Bulut et al. (2022) pp. 8–10.
[53] Bulut et al. (2022) p. 8.
[54] Bulut et al. (2022) p. 10.

semantically integrating the data with BIRD's reference code, column names are standardized across both reports.[55] Semantic integration aims to integrate definitions and of different data dictionaries into one reporting frameworks. As a result, international reporting concepts with the same meaning are uniquely named and defined.[56] This unified approach ensures a shared data foundation for (Fig. 4.18)

SHS REFERENCE

DT_RFRNC	ISIN	CNTRY_ISSR	TYP_INSTRMNT	ORGNL_MTRTY	MRKT_VL
Reference date	ISIN code	Country of the Issuer	Type of Instrument	Original maturity	Market value
31/12/2016	XX1234567	DE	210 (Debt instrument)	2 (Short term)	2000
31/12/2016	XX9876543	DE	317 (Equity Instrument)	0 (not applicable)	900

CSDB REFERENCE

DT_RFRNC	ISIN	CNTRY_ISSR	TYP_INSTRMNT	ORGNL_MTRTY	MRKT_VL
Reference date	ISIN code	Country of the Issuer	Type of Instrument	Original maturity	Market value
31/01/2017	XX1234567	DE	210 (Debt instrument)	2 (Short term)	2200
31/01/2017	XX9876543	DE	317 (Equity Instrument)	0 (not applicable)	3000

Fig. 4.18 Example with semantic integration[57]

various reports, eliminating the need to search for and re-enter information when transitioning between reports.[58]

4.3.4 BIRD and the Austrian Model

The Basic Cube has, in part, served as a model for the BIRD system. Both systems are intended for voluntary adoption. But still, the Austrian data model differs significantly from the BIRD initiative in some key respects. One major difference lies in the reporting structure approaches. While the BIRD output layer is centred on secondary reporting, which reflects the data transmitted by the central banks to the ECB, the Austrian data model is centred on primary reporting, in which

[55] Bulut et al. (2022) p. 10.

[56] European Banking Authority (2021) p. 34.

[57] Bulut et al. (2022) p. 11.

[58] Bulut et al. (2022) p. 10.

the commercial banks transmit their data directly to the OeNB. This distinction results from the lack of a harmonised primary reporting system at European level.

Another notable difference lies in the handling of validation rules. In BIRD, validation rules are integral to ensuring data consistency at the input layer and they are well-documented. Conversely, in the Austrian data model, the validation of the input layer is primarily delegated to banks or service providers.

In terms of the content covered, the BIRD documentation is currently still overshadowed by the Austrian data model, which covers more reporting requirements. Another difference is the complete formal mapping of the BIRD content, which enables automated extraction of the content, whereas this is not possible in the Austrian data model.

The ECB's IReF project is running in parallel to the BIRD initiative and aims to create a standardized basis for the format and structure of reports that is as redundancy-free as possible. Major synergy effects could be achieved by interlinking the results of BIRD, the Austrian Basic Cube and IReF, as IReF represents a harmonised reporting scheme for primary reporting on which BIRD can build.

4.3.5 Examples of BIRD

The BIRD serves as a guide for banks as it provides standardized templates, data definitions and reporting guidelines that banks can follow. When browsing prudential frameworks like FINREP in BIRD, users would interact with SMCubes to access the structured data elements and annotations that provide guidance on what to report and how to report it within the FINREP framework. BIRD categorizes two concepts, the reference and the non-reference category. Reference concepts are characterized by a unique codification system, known as the BIRD, with the ECB serving as the maintenance agency. One of BIRD's objectives is to establish a distinct set of codes to represent these concepts. Non-reference concepts are described using original codes, belonging to their own codification system and are maintained by entities other than the ECB, for example, EBA for FINREP.[59] The ROL utilizes reference codes derived from the BIRD lexicon to describe regulatory reporting requirements. In contrast, the NROL employs non-reference codes from the EBA DPM for the same purpose. The reference codes serve as a standardized language across all BIRD layers.[60]

---

[59] European Central Bank (n. d. b) n.pag.

[60] Bulut et al. (2022) pp. 6–10.

4.3.6 Example FINREP

1. Balance Sheet Statement [Statement of Financial Position]

1.1 Assets

		References	Breakdown in table	Carrying amount
				Annex V.Part 1.27
				010
010	**Cash, cash balances at central banks and other demand deposits**	*IAS 1.54 (i)*		
020	Cash on hand	*Annex V.Part 2.1*		
030	Cash balances at central banks	*Annex V.Part 2.2*		
040	Other demand deposits	*Annex V.Part 2.3*	5	
050	**Financial assets held for trading**	*IFRS 9.Appendix A*		
060	Derivatives	*IFRS 9.Appendix A*	10	
070	Equity instruments	*IAS 32.11*	4	
080	Debt securities	*Annex V.Part 1.31*	4	
090	Loans and advances	*Annex V.Part 1.32*	4	

Fig. 4.19 FINREP template[61]

BIRD offers guidance to banks regarding accurate data reporting through a dedicated website known as the BIRD navigator. Once the FINREP reference is located, users can find descriptions of all templates from the FINREP report presented in a consistent manner. For instance, the identifier "Code: 112718_REF" serves as the standardized name for "cash on hand," with "020" indicating the identical cash on hand within the template. "F 01.01" specifically points to the corresponding table that includes assets. By clicking on the reference link opens a comprehensive description containing all the necessary requirements, providing guidance to the user. BIRD offers taxonomies that translate business requirements into XBRL format and contain definitions of reportable requirements (Figs. 4.19 and 4.20).

In this example we got the following taxonomy:

EBA_APL(EBA_PL_EBA_x12)|EBA_ATY(EBA_mi53)|EBA_BAS(EBA_BA_EBA_x6)|EBA_CPS(EBA_CT_EBA_x0)|EBA_MCY(EBA_MC_EBA_x44[62]

[61] European Banking Authority (n.d.a) n.pag.

[62] European Central Bank (2024) n.pag.

Template Representation

F 01.01 Balance Sheet Statement [Statement of Financial Position]: Assets (F_01.01_REF)

Y axis		X axis: Carrying amount
		0010
Cash, cash balances at central banks and other dem...	0010	10898_REF
Cash on hand	0020	112718_REF
Cash balances at central banks	0030	151111_REF
Other demand deposits	0040	151115_REF
Financial assets held for trading	0050	11110_REF
Derivatives	0060	11108_REF
Equity instruments	0070	11112_REF
Debt securities	0080	11106_REF
Loans and advances	0090	11114_REF

Fig. 4.20 Representation of FINREP in the BIRD navigator[63]

- EBA_APL(EBA_PL_EBA_x12): This code refers to cash and cash equivalents held by a financial institution, such as funds deposited in central banks and other demand deposit accounts. It's a measure of liquidity.
- EBA_ATY(EBA_mi53): This code represents the carrying amount of a specific type of asset, possibly stock or inventory, denoted as stock "i". The term "monetary m" might indicate that it involves financial assets.
- EBA_BAS(EBA_BA_EBA_x6): This code refers to the category of assets held by a financial institution. It could encompass various types of assets such as loans, securities and physical assets.
- EBA_CPS(EBA_CT_EBA_x0): This code indicates that the item is not applicable or that it encompasses all base items.
- EBA_MCY(EBA_MC_EBA_x44): This code refers to the amount of cash held on hand by a financial institution. It could include physical currency as well as cash equivalents readily accessible for day-to-day operations.

[63] European Central Bank (2024a) n.pag.

4.3.7 Example SHSG

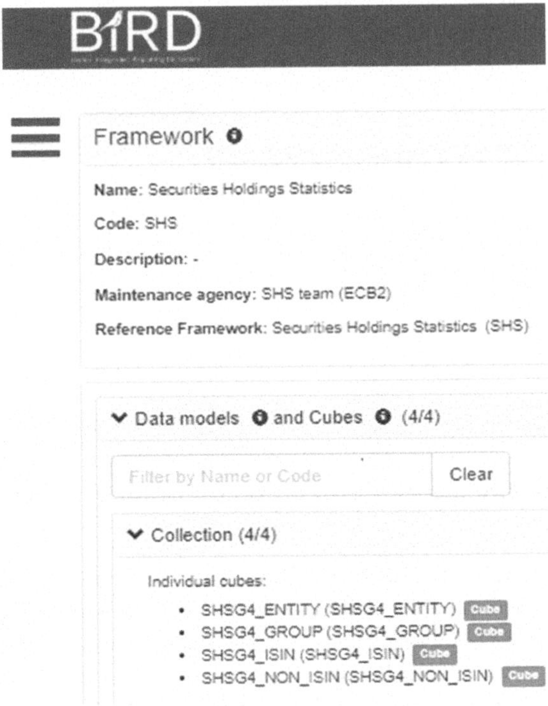

Fig. 4.21 Overview of SHS in the BIRD navigator[64]

Within the SHS, the SHS branches out further into different categories, namely: SHS-Entity, SHS-Group, SHS-ISIN and SHS-NON-ISIN. When navigating through the BIRD, users can easily distinguish between these different sets of templates. In particular, the SHS-Group, abbreviated as SHSG, is shown in Fig. 4.21 and provides a comprehensive overview of the reporting obligations, which is also accessible via Excel. In combination with the BIRD navigator, the user can find a comprehensive guideline for the reporting requirements (Figs. 4.22 and 4.23).

[64] European Central Bank (2024a) n.pag.

Fig. 4.22 Cube representation[65]

By selecting the "Observations" in the BIRD navigator, the user can view the description of the reporting requirements. For the field FREQ, the user can see the reporting frequency described as quarterly. For COMPILING_ORG, all national banks are listed. Via the BIRD interface, employees have immediate access to detailed descriptions of the templates, so they know exactly the data requirements for each reporting obligation, consequently increasing the speed and understanding of regulatory reporting.

4.3.8 Example AnaCredit

The AnaCredit framework was incorporated into BIRD without requiring methodological integration, as the AnaCredit metadata were directly developed within the SMCube methodology (Fig. 4.24).[66]

---

[65] European Central Bank (2024a) n.pag.

[66] European Central Bank (2019) p. 64.

SHS Group Reporting scheme - holder information data on Group level

Colors:
Attributes for the preceding dimensions/values
Dimension, part of key
Annotations (remarks, codes...)

1. Header Information

csv column number	*Header Element*	*Short Name*
1	Reporting institution code	COMPILING_ORG
2	Time Period	PERIOD
3	Frequency	FREQ

2. Holdings information

csv column number	*Attribute or dimension*	*Short Name*
4	Type of Input for group	INPUT_TYPE_GROUP
5	**Group ID**	**GROUP_ID**
6	**Group ID type**	**GROUP_ID_TYPE**
7	Group LEI	GROUP_LEI
8	Group type	GROUP_TYPE
9	ESA 2010 Sector of the head of group	GROUP_SECTOR
10	Name of the Reporting Group	GROUP_NAME
11	Accounting Standard of the Group	GROUP_ACC_STANDARD

Fig. 4.23 SHSG template[67]

[67] European Central Bank (n.d.c) n.pag.

Fig. 4.24 Overview of AnaCredit in the BIRD navigator[68]

The AnaCredit comprises nine segments that the supervised banks are required to report. Each category further divides into more detailed subsections. The financial data segment, seen in Fig. 4.25, further splits into 16 reportable components.

[68] European Central Bank (2024a) n.pag.

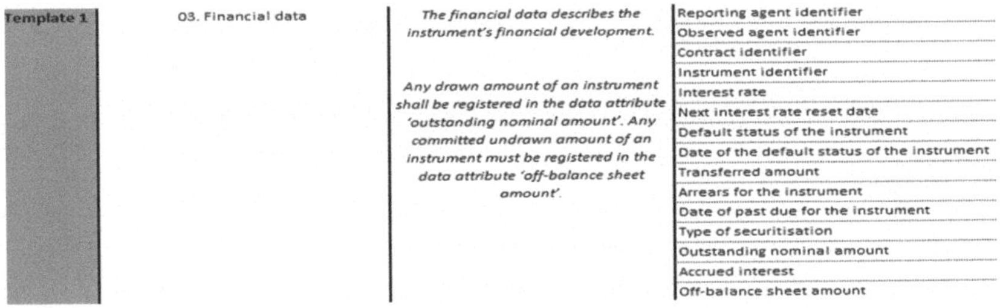

Fig. 4.25 AnaCredit template[69]

These components and their respective constraints for their values are accessible through the BIRD navigator, supporting banks in ensuring accurate and consistent regulatory reporting processes (Fig. 4.26).

4.4 IReF

Over the last ten years, national and international regulatory reporting has intensified dramatically. As a result, the cost of reporting has almost doubled for both the institutions and the authorities as illustrated in Fig. 4.27. This increase can be attributed to the diverse and growing reporting requirements over the years. Financial institutions often provide redundant data due not having integrated reporting systems. To make matters worse, more and more granular data collections are required which further increases the reporting burden for financial institutions.[70]

Given the challenges posed by statistical, prudential and national reporting requirements, the IReF aims to integrate and harmonise reporting requirements for European banks and consequently, standardize data collection and transformation processes by introducing a semantically integrated and redundancy-free collection layer.[71] The ECB is planning to introduce an IReF regulation that will define the statistical data requirements that apply directly to banks in the eurozone. Non-euro area EU member states have the option to adopt IReF reporting either fully or partially through national legislation, potentially incorporating elements related to AnaCredit, for instance. The implementation of IReF

[69] European Central Bank (n.d.a) n.pag.

[70] Freund/Gutsche (2022) p. 1.

[71] European Central Bank (n.d.e) n.pag.

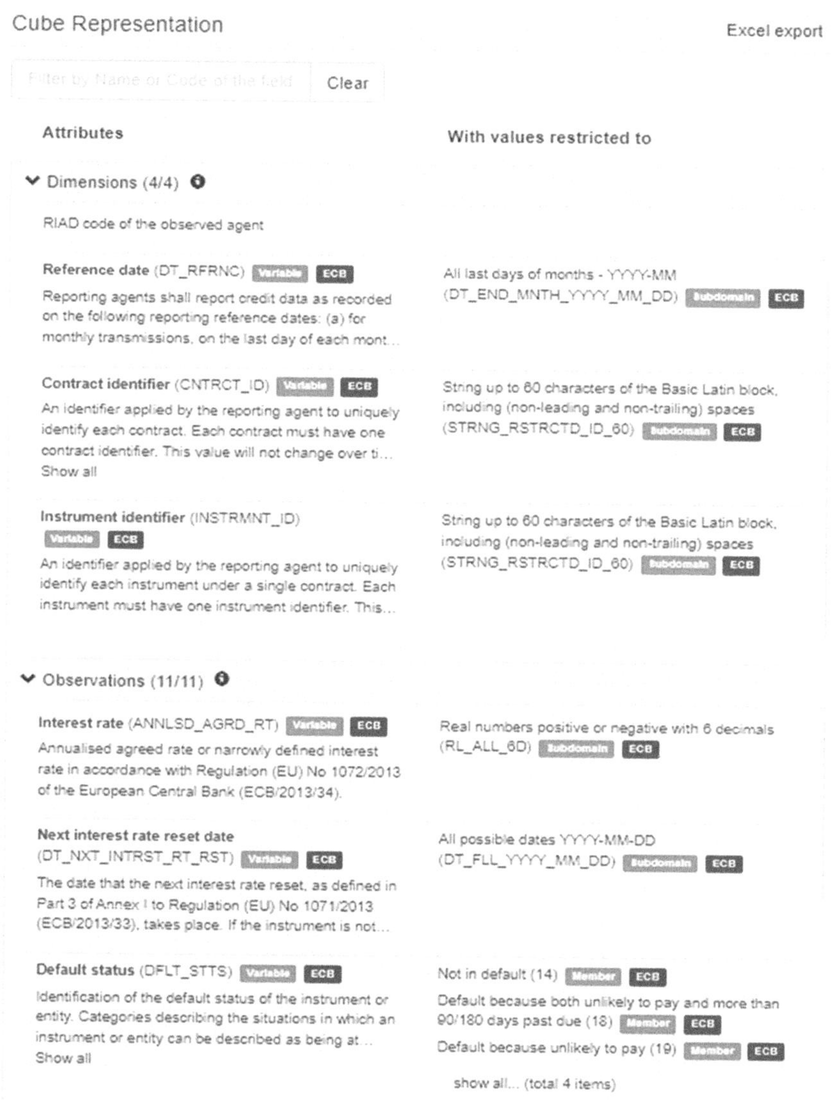

Fig. 4.26 Cube representation[72]

[72] European Central Bank (2024a) n.pag.

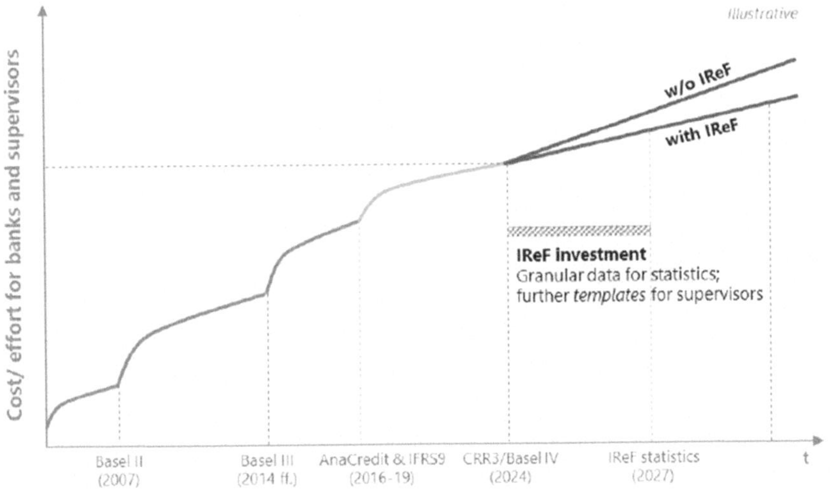

Fig. 4.27 Waves of cost in regulatory reporting[73]

holds promise for strengthening the banking and monetary union. Through cross-country standardization of reporting, it may help mitigate barriers that often hinder smaller banks from engaging in cross-border operations, thereby encouraging greater competition within the EU financial sector. Cost efficiency under IReF is anticipated through economies of scale and the consistent application of the "define once, report once, regulate once, perform as one system" principle.[74]

IReF streamlines banks' statistical reporting needs into a singular framework directly applicable to euro area banks. It is expected that the collection layer eliminates the need for translation into national collection frameworks like the Austrian Basic Cube. With its standardised data model, IReF will ensure an integrated and harmonised regulatory reporting system and thus enable redundancy-free data transmission despite high granularity requirements.[75]

The implementation of the IReF will bring significant benefits to reporting entities. Reporting requirements will be structured based on a logical data model, with data collection based on standardized implementation methods. A common data dictionary will ensure consistency of definitions, while reporting frequency,

---

[73] Freund/Gutsche (2022) p. 1.

[74] European Central Bank (2022) pp. 2–8.

[75] Colangelo et al. (2021) p. 8.

deadlines and granularity will be uniformly standardized. The framework will establish a common set of data quality rules, including validation, that apply to all actors, as well as a revision policy. Internationally active banks are expected to be the main beneficiaries of IReF, as the semantic integration will eliminate redundancies and reporting errors, but smaller banks will also feel an impact as supervisory reporting is expected to stabilise over time. The frequency of ad hoc requests for information is likely to decrease and a higher degree of standardization will facilitate the adoption of standard IT solutions. While initial investment may be required, ongoing costs are likely to decrease due to the standardized requirements and improved granularity under the IReF system. In the medium to long term, banks will derive additional benefits from the integration of statistical, regulatory and settlement requirements. These aspects will be analyzed in detail as part of a transparent cost-benefit analysis involving all IReF stakeholders. Central bank statisticians will also benefit as they will only receive one set of statistical data to produce the datasets covered by the IReF. Standardized data models will ensure methodological soundness and compliance with statistical standards, while integrated data collection can create opportunities for further automation of statistical production and dissemination systems. IReF will promote the use of statistical data, by ensuring precise and clear definitions of the relevant statistical data. This will increase data accuracy and comparability across datasets and countries, thereby improving the quality and analytical value of the data obtained. In addition, the availability of detailed data on loans and securities will enable policy makers, banks, academics and the public to analyse economic and financial trends more quickly and comprehensively (Fig. 4.28).[76]

[76] European Central Bank (2022) pp. 4–8.

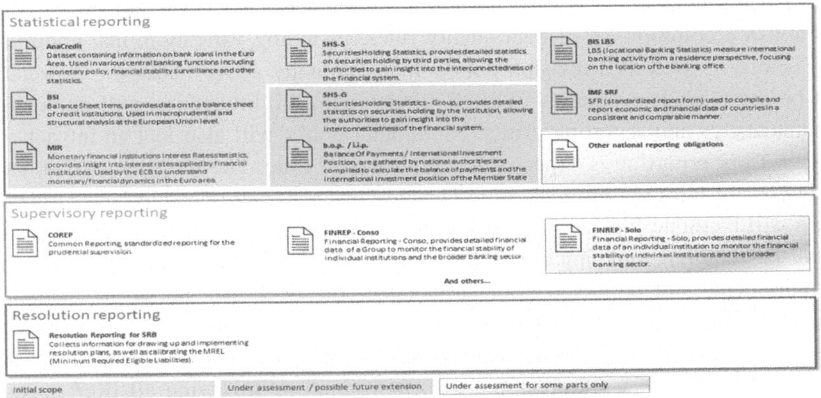

Fig. 4.28 IReF's intial scope[77]

The IReF's initial scope encompasses the AnaCredit, BSI, MIR and SHS-S reporting requirements. As it progresses, the IReF will introduce additional reporting mandates in the foreseeable future. The release of IReF is scheduled for 2027.[78] Fig. 4.29 underscores the importance of integrating supplementary reporting requirements into the system to fully leverage the benefits of IReF.[79]

In November 2020, the ESCB in cooperation with the banking sector and participating member states, carried out a comprehensive cost-benefit evaluation to estimate the potential benefit of the IReF. By April 2021, the results were showing strong support for integrating supervisory reporting in the Eurozone. In addition, the study concluded that the reduction in reporting costs would outweigh the initial investment for the introduction of the IReF in the long term. Following this initial assessment, the ESCB initiated a complementary cost-benefit assessment, which started in May 2023 and was finalized in February 2024. In particular, the possibility of including country-specific statistical reporting requirements in the IReF regulation was assessed. Currently, the EU is in the process of drafting an ECB regulation pertaining to the IReF. This draft regulation will undergo a public consultation before being adapted.[80]

---

[77] Dessalles (2023) n.pag.

[78] Dessalles (2023) n.pag.

[79] Freund/Gutsche (2022) p. 16.

[80] European Central Bank (n.d.e) n.pag.

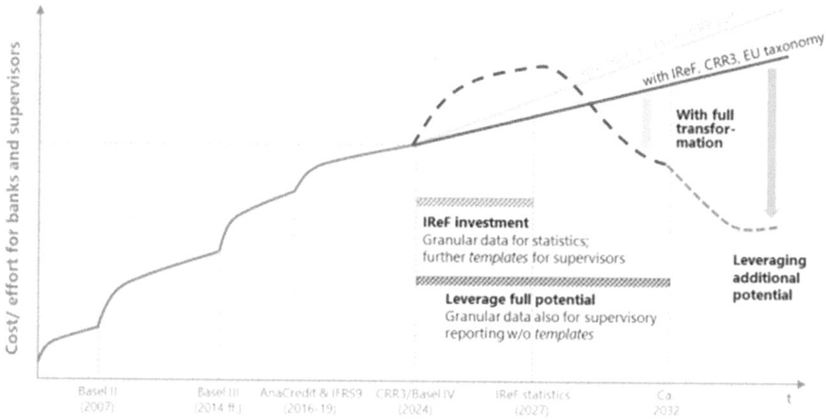

Fig. 4.29 Cost reduction with full transformation[81]

4.4.1 Methodology

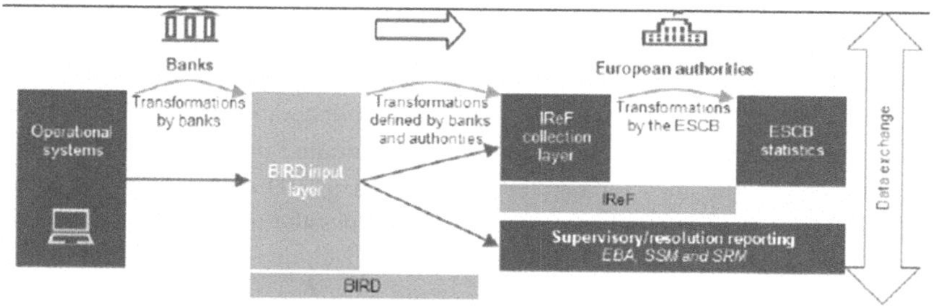

Fig. 4.30 Integrated reporting in the Eurozone[82]

In the current version, the BIRD and the IReF initiative have been linked together as they are using the same metadata provided by the SDD. The link between these initiatives is facilitated by aligning the IReF collection layer and the BIRD input layer as seen on Fig. 4.30. This establishes the connection

[81] Freund/Gutsche (2022) p. 16.

[82] Colangelo et al. (2021) p. 9.

between BIRD and ESCB statistics and illustrates the practical utility of the initiative for banks and supervision. The IReF collection layer contains granular data that must be reported to supervisors alongside aggregated reports. This allows supervisors to use this data not only for report preparation but also for further, deeper analysis. Within the collection layer, the data undergoes processing according to transformation rules at the ESCB level, ultimately resulting in the generation of statistics.[83] BIRD specifies the process of transforming data from banks' internal source systems into a predefined data model, essentially mapping bank-specific data onto the regulatory taxonomy. Within the bank, the refined, granular data is gathered in the format of the BIRD data model before being submitted to the European supervisory authority following the bank's transformation. When coupled with IReF, this ideally streamlines the provision of granular data, requiring only one submission per reporting period in the IReF collection layer. Subsequently, the supervisory authority generates the necessary statistics using defined transformation protocols.[84]

4.4.2 IReF and BIRD

Combining the BIRD and the IReF is essential for achieving the objectives of implementing a harmonised and integrated reporting framework within the EU. BIRD expands upon IReF by encompassing the broader reporting spectrum, addressing both supervisory and resolution requirements. Unlike IReF, BIRD isn't a regulatory mandate nor legally binding. It's a collaborative effort between the ESCB and the banking sector aimed at crafting a unified data framework, model and conversion guidelines for regulatory reporting. BIRD defines the data to be sourced from banks' internal IT systems and outlines the transformation process to produce requisite reports. By providing a centralized dictionary and conversion rules, BIRD facilitates consistency in reporting, ensuring banks deliver uniform, high-quality data. This streamlines supervisory tasks and eases the reporting burden on banks. IReF and BIRD are designed to complement each other, with IReF serving as the statistical component embedded within BIRD, covering supervisory and resolution reporting as well.[85]

---

[83] Kloos et al. (2022) n.pag.

[84] Müller (2020) n.pag.

[85] Dessalles (2023) n.pag.

Two important considerations explain how the IReF is aligned with the BIRD. BIRD and IReF are making use of the same reference codification system. Further, the IReF has a particularly high level of granularity and detail to achieve integration via a relational model and avoid redundancies. Consequently, it is much more closely aligned with the IL/EIL structure than other reporting requirements, both in terms of modelling and content. It is therefore advisable to harmonise the data models of IReF and BIRD. An ongoing issue for the IReF is the consideration national reporting requirements. The aim is to minimize the country-specific requirements, but some national reporting requirements will remain within the IReF. For this purpose, the ECB plans to develop an so-called extended IReF layer to model and describe these remaining country-specific requirements. This approach would help reporting agents by ensuring a harmonised description of overlapping requirements across countries. It is intended that the ECB regulation for the IReF will cover the common reporting requirements, such for statistical reporting, while national legislation will deal with country-specific requirements. By combining BIRD and IReF, additional reporting frameworks can be implemented seamlessly. IReF and BIRD share a common entity, though IReF doesn't require the entirety of the EIL content. In other words, IReF is a subset of BIRD and BIRD is therefore an extension of IReF (Fig. 4.31).[86]

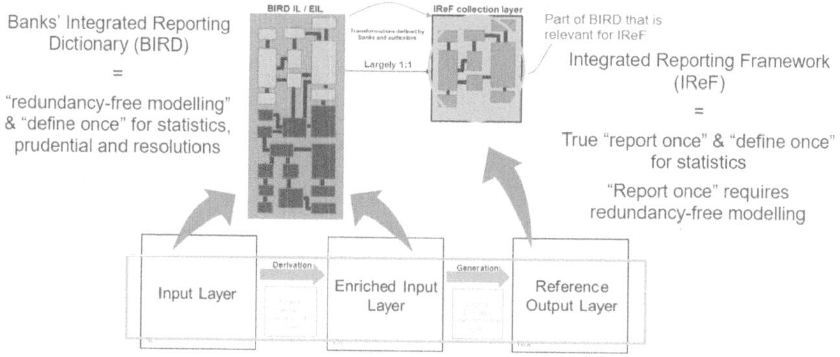

Fig. 4.31 Alignment of BIRD and IReF[87]

[86] Colangelo et al. (2021) n.pag.

[87] European Central Bank (2024a) n.pag.

Analysis of the Expert Interviews 5

This chapter deals with the findings of the expert interviews. The results help to validate the evidence from the literature review and the case studies with the practical expertise of experts who are directly involved in the development and implementation of reporting standards at the European Central Bank and the Austrian National Bank. The presentation of these findings is structured according to the categories outlined in the qualitative content analysis methodology discussed in the previous section and is designed to answer the hypotheses and ultimately the research question.

5.1 Current Trends

Since the financial crisis, regulatory reporting is undergoing a substantially development. As data requirements become more detailed and the scope of reporting obligations continues to grow, the need for harmonised and integrated regulatory reporting is more important than ever. Initiatives of the ECB and the EBA are intended to harmonise reporting and, with the introduction of IReF and BIRD, are seen as a significant step towards harmonised supervisory reporting. At the same time, the level of complexity is increasing.

5.2 Opportunities of Integrated Systems

In response to these challenges, new regulatory reporting frameworks such as IReF and BIRD are emerging. These frameworks have been developed to meet the evolving landscape of supervisory reporting, which is characterised by the need for more detailed data. By implementing an integrated reporting system,

D. Dorrer, *Introduction of IReF*, BestMasters,
https://doi.org/10.1007/978-3-658-46447-9_5

semantic integration can be achieved, reducing the reporting burden, particularly for cross-border banks. In addition, an integrated system can effectively eliminate redundancies in reporting, as overlapping data is automatically consolidated and transferred to the required reports. BIRD is designed as a data dictionary to help banks determine the data requirements when submitting regulatory reports, while IReF aims to streamline statistical supervisory reporting.

5.3 Challenges with Integrated Systems

The complexity associated with the introduction of new supervisory reporting frameworks represents a considerable challenge. Harmonising these frameworks into a uniform system requires substantial resources and effort. There are currently various national and international regulatory requirements and merging them into a harmonised framework will be a lengthy process that will take several years. One possible solution for understanding this complicated reporting landscape is the introduction of BIRD as a data dictionary. The BIRD can serve as a guide to help users navigate the complexity of reporting requirements. In addition, there is an urgent need for solutions that allow national reporting frameworks such as the Basic Cube to be seamlessly integrated into the new frameworks.

5.4 BIRD and IReF

A synergy between BIRD and IReF can be used to streamline reporting procedures. The BIRD serves as a comprehensive data dictionary that describes the data requirements for reporting within the IReF framework in a harmonised way. However, it should be noted that BIRD can be challenging for beginners due to its complexity. Nonetheless, the integration of BIRD into IReF offers the potential to increase data consistency, improve reporting accuracy and facilitate compliance with regulatory standards.

5.5 IReF

The IReF methodology aims to collect data across the eurozone in a standardized way. It can be seen as a starting point from which the necessary data for the international level can be derived. This standardized model passes on the data automatically and without redundancies for the compilation of various statistics.

This model can therefore be compared with the Austrian Basic Cube, as it works in a similar way by using smart cubes. By introducing a harmonized system, the current way of reporting in the Eurozone can be unified, as not every member state has a collection framework like the Austrian Basic Cube.

5.6 Future Implications

The adoption of the IReF represents a remarkable progress in the standardization and harmonisation of supervisory reporting practices across the Eurozone. This framework aims to improve transparency, consistency and efficiency in reporting processes. However, concerns have emerged regarding the compatibility of existing national reporting systems, such as the Austrian Basic Cube, with this new framework. The Austrian Basic Cube is a foundational concept in integrated reporting within the Eurozone. It serves as the national supervisory reporting concept for reporting obligations, ensuring consistency in the data submitted by banks to regulatory authorities. Its establishment laid the groundwork for subsequent initiatives such as the BIRD, further advancing reporting standardization and harmonisation. Interviews with experts highlight the similarities between the two frameworks, emphasizing their common goal of creating an integrated and harmonised reporting framework. While experts recognize the potential benefits of the Basic Cube in conjunction with IReF, they also acknowledge the complexities involved, particularly considering IReF's gradual implementation over the coming years.

In the short term, the transition of the Basic Cube into the IReF framework involves replacing the Smart Cubes for statistical reporting, while retaining the Basic Cube for national reporting obligations or prudential reporting. This transition will be facilitated by the application of transformation rules that adapt the data collected in the Basic Cube to meet the reporting requirements of IReF, including AnaCredit, BSI, MIR and SHS. Looking ahead, the long-term strategy involves the gradual dissolution of the Basic Cube for additional reporting obligations through the implementation of so-called International Extended Technical Layers. However, the specific direction of this evolution remains uncertain and will depend on future developments. Another possibility is maintaining the Basic Cube as a national collection system that transfers data for IReF obligations, allowing it to coexist and complement the new framework. Experts caution that integrating the Basic Cube into IReF requires careful planning to minimize disruptions to existing reporting practices. They stress the importance of ensuring compatibility and coordination between the two frameworks. Some experts express concerns about potential challenges during the transition period, emphasizing the need for strategic planning and collaboration among national and international systems and authorities.

5.7 Impact on Risk Management Practices, Regulatory Compliance and Overall Financial Stability

The implementation of integrated regulatory frameworks leads to semantic integration, resulting in better comparability and consistency, which reduces the reporting volume and the associated costs. This shift away from the traditional isolated reporting departments within national banks towards more integrated structures increases efficiency. Integrated systems streamline the reporting process and facilitate compliance, particularly with the help of BIRD, which simplifies reporting tasks for employees in the reporting departments of commercial banks. In addition, the use of IReF enables the effortless compilation of multiple statistics, giving the ECB a broader overview and allowing it to manage risk effectively. By promoting an integrated approach to reporting standards, regulatory bodies can better manage systemic risks and respond more quickly to emerging challenges. This increased oversight not only strengthens investor confidence but also improves financial institutions' resilience to financial uncertainty. Additionally, the adoption of integrated policies fosters collaboration and knowledge sharing between regulators, facilitating coordinated responses to ongoing market dynamics. Overall, the introduction of integrated supervisory frameworks will not only streamline reporting procedures, but also improve compliance and risk management capabilities across the banking sector, thereby enhancing financial stability in the Eurozone.

Conclusion 6

The introduction of integrated reporting frameworks, such as the Banks' Integrated Reporting Dictionary and the Integrated Reporting Framework, represents a significant step forward in the European banking sector's efforts to achieve integrated, harmonised and efficient supervisory reporting practices. Through an in-depth analysis of these frameworks, this master's thesis is dedicated to answering the following research questionThe introduction of integrated reporting frameworks, such as the Banks' Integrated Reporting Dictionary and the Integrated Reporting Framework, represents a significant step forward in the European banking sector's efforts to achieve integrated, harmonised and efficient supervisory reporting practices. Through an in-depth analysis of these frameworks, this master's thesis is dedicated to answering the following research question:

> *"What impact does the harmonisation of reporting standards at the European Central Bank, through the introduction of the Integrated Reporting Framework (IReF) system and the establishment of the Banks' Integrated Reporting Dictionary (BIRD), have on risk management practices, regulatory compliance and overall financial stability among various financial institutions operating in the Eurozone?"*

Through the research conducted in this master's thesis, it has become evident that both BIRD and IReF have played instrumental roles in simplifying reporting processes, reducing reporting burdens, enhancing data quality and comparability across different datasets and countries. By providing standardized templates, data definitions and reporting guidelines, BIRD has facilitated greater transparency, accuracy and efficiency in reporting practices. Meanwhile, the impending introduction of IReF is expected to bring significant changes in the regulatory reporting landscape. Its comprehensive approach to integrating and harmonising

D. Dorrer, *Introduction of IReF*, BestMasters,
https://doi.org/10.1007/978-3-658-46447-9_6

reporting requirements for European banks will not only streamline data collection and reporting processes, but also enable institutions such as the ECB or EBA to make decisions and analyse economic and financial trends more accurately, thereby improving financial stability in the Eurozone. Moreover, by linking these initiatives together, banks will benefit from possible synergies arising from using the BIRD and the IReF, resulting in cost savings, improved data quality and enhanced regulatory compliance. The connection between BIRD and IReF, will enable banks to submit granular data to European supervisory authorities efficiently, reducing redundancies and consequently enhancing regulatory oversight and analysis capabilities. Moreover, the incorporation of the Austrian Basic Cube into the IReF framework highlights the importance of aligning national reporting systems with European-wide initiatives. While the Basic Cube serves as a foundational concept in integrated reporting within Austria, its integration with IReF will require careful planning and coordination to ensure compatibility and consistency across reporting practices. Strategic planning and collaboration among regulatory authorities, financial institutions and national central banks will be crucial in minimizing disruptions and maximizing the benefits of this introduction of supervisory systems.

Looking ahead, the full implementation of IReF in the Eurozone in 2027 will mark a significant milestone in the journey towards integrating and harmonising regulatory reporting practices across the European banking sector. As banks transition to the new reporting framework, they will need to adapt their internal systems and processes to comply with the standardized data models, guidelines and reporting schedules outlined in IReF. While there may be challenges during the transition period, the long-term benefits of IReF, including cost savings, improved data quality and enhanced regulatory oversight, will outweigh the initial implementation costs.

Given the prolonged implementation period of IReF, currently planned concepts are subject to change. Therefore, this master's thesis can only provide an overview of the current status of integrated supervisory reporting and the proposed plans for a harmonized reporting system. It is important to acknowledge that as the implementation progresses, adjustments and refinements to these concepts may occur. However, while the full impact of IReF can only be accurately assessed once it is fully operational, it is evident that its introduction will significantly influence current reporting practices and the surrounding fields. As IReF gradually becomes operational, it is expected to bring about notable changes in regulatory reporting procedures, operational frameworks, and compliance standards within the financial sector.

In conclusion, the harmonisation of reporting standards at the ECB through the introduction of IReF and the establishment of BIRD has and will continue to have a transformative effect on risk management practices, regulatory compliance and overall financial stability in the Eurozone. These initiatives have laid the foundation for a more integrated, transparent and efficient reporting ecosystem, thereby contributing to the stability, resilience and competitiveness of the European banking sector.

References

Adeoye-Olatunde, O. / Olenik, N. (2021): Research and scholarly methods: Semi-structured interviews, in: JACCP: JOURNAL OF THE AMERICAN COLLEGE OF CLINICAL PHARMACY, 4/10, pp. 1358–1367

Arru, D. / Oddone, G. (2022): Defining business transformation rules in a standardised format–a practical case, retrieved from https://ideas.repec.org/h/bis/bisifc/59-31.html, accessed March 22, 2024

Basias, N. / Pollalis, Y. (2018): Quantitative and qualitative research in business & technology: Justifying a suitable research methodology, in: Review of Integrative Business and Economics Research, 7, pp. 91–105, retrieved from https://sibresearch.org/uploads/3/4/0/9/34097180/riber_7-s1_sp_h17-083_91-105.pdf, accessed April 19, 2024

Beck, T. (2024): Cross-border supervisory cooperation: a progress report and research agenda, in: SSRN Electronic Journal, retrieved from https://papers.ssrn.com/sol3/papers.cfm?abstract_id=4769336, accessed April 11, 2024

Bellairs, C. / Bradley, V. (2022): What Is FINREP?, retrieved from https://www.bdo.co.uk/en-gb/insights/industries/financial-services/what-is-finrep, accessed April 15, 2024

Benczur, P. / Cannas, G. / Cariboni, J. / Di Girolamo, F. / Maccaferri, S. / Petracco Giudici, M. (2017): Evaluating the effectiveness of the new EU bank regulatory framework: A farewell to bail-out?, in: Journal of Financial Stability, 33, pp. 207–223, retrieved from https://www.sciencedirect.com/science/article/pii/S1572308916300018, accessed April 2, 2024

Blaschke, J. / Witt, E. (2018): ECB data for analysis and decision-making: data governance and technology, retrieved from https://www.bis.org/ifc/publ/ifcb49_36.pdf, accessed April 15, 2024

Boermans, M. (2022): A literature review of securities holdings statistics research and a practitioner's guide, in: SSRN Electronic Journal, retrieved from https://papers.ssrn.com/sol3/papers.cfm?abstract_id=4304056, accessed April 9, 2024

Boixo, I. (2012): The Data Point Model methodology in the European Supervision: COREP/FINREP, retrieved from https://www.eurofiling.info/documents/DataPointModelMethodologyIB.pdf, accessed February 17, 2024

Bulut, P. / Knape, M. / Steßl, R. (2022): BIRD and IReF - Towards an Integrated Reporting System, retrieved from https://www.finbridge.de/trends/2022/08/29/bird-and-iref, accessed February 21, 2024

D. Dorrer, *Introduction of IReF*, BestMasters,
https://doi.org/10.1007/978-3-658-46447-9

Cech, C. / Helmreich, S. (eds.) (2017): Meldewesen für Finanzinstitute. Was bringt die neue europäische Aufsicht?, SpringerLink Bücher, Wiesbaden: Springer Gabler

Challapalli, S. (2023): Benefits and Constraints Associated with the Harmonization of Financial Regulations: An Overview, in: Asian Journal of Economics, Business and Accounting, 23.15, pp. 49–56, retrieved from https://papers.ssrn.com/sol3/papers.cfm?abstract_id=4473299, accessed April 8, 2024

Chiti, M. (2019): The Palgrave Handbook of European Banking Union Law, Cham: Palgrave Macmillan US, retrieved from https://ebookcentral.proquest.com/lib/kxp/detail.action?docID=5776165, accessed February 17, 2024

Chopra, R. (2010): Database management systems (DBMS). A practical approach : concepts, principles, case studies, experiments, New Delhi: S. Chand

Clifford, C. (2017): EU Regulatory Developments, in: Law and Financial Markets Review, 11/2-3, pp. 143–149

Colangelo, A. / Gross, F. / Schuster, F. (2021): Effective measurement of the economy in the emerging digital age, in: Proceedings 63rd ISI World Statistics Congress, 11, retrieved from https://www.isi-web.org/sites/default/files/import/pdf/202-day4-ips213-effective-measurement-of-the-e.pdf, accessed March 12, 2024

Coronel, C. / Morris, S. (2019): Database systems. Design, implementation, and management, retrieved from https://thuvienso.hoasen.edu.vn/handle/123456789/9321, accessed March 19, 2024

Cusano, F. / Marinelli, G. / Piermattei, S. (2021): Learning from Revisions: A Tool for Detecting Potential Errors in Banks' Balance Sheet Statistical Reporting, in: SSRN Electronic Journal, retrieved from https://papers.ssrn.com/sol3/papers.cfm?abstract_id=3852249, accessed April 9, 2024

Dessalles, Q. (2023): BIRD and IReF, the simplification of banks' reporting?, retrieved from https://www.linkedin.com/pulse/bird-iref-simplification-banks-reporting-quentin-dessalles/, accessed February 27, 2024

Eurofiling (n.d.): Data Point Model, REFERENCES ABOUT DATA POINT MODELLING (DPM), retrieved from https://eurofiling.info/portal/data-point-model/, accessed February 17, 2024

Eurofiling (2009): Data Points Structure Explanatory Documentation, retrieved from https://www.eurofiling.info/finrepTaxonomy/taxonomy/DataPointsStructureExplanatoryDocumentation20091208v02.pdf, accessed February 19, 2024

European Banking Authority (n. d. a): Implementing Technical Standards on amendments to FINREP due to IFRS 9, retrieved from https://www.eba.europa.eu/implementing-technical-standards-amendments-finrep-due-ifrs-9, accessed April 11, 2024

European Banking Authority (n. d. b): The Single Rulebook, retrieved from https://www.eba.europa.eu/single-rulebook, accessed February 6, 2024

European Banking Authority (2011): Corep-reporting-framework, retrieved from https://www.eba.europa.eu/sites/default/files/documents/10180/62404/066fb0c8-bdc9-4c7c-9b45-a94f20998822/Corep-reporting-framework.pdf, accessed March 28, 2024

European Banking Authority (2014): Abstract description of the model represented in taxonomies following the DPM approach, February 17, 2024, retrieved from https://www.eurofiling.info/finrepTaxonomy/DPM-Formal-Model.pdf, accessed March 5, 2024

European Banking Authority (2021): Discussion Paper, On a Feasibility Study of an Integrated Reporting System under Article 430c CRR, retrieved from https://www.eba.eur

opa.eu/publications-and-media/events/discussion-feasibility-study-integrated-reporting-system-under, accessed February 22, 2024
European Central Bank (n. d. a): AnaCredit, retrieved from https://www.ecb.europa.eu/stats/ecb_statistics/anacredit/html/index.en.html, accessed April 11, 2024
European Central Bank (n. d. b): BIRD navigator, retrieved from https://bird.ecb.europa.eu/userguide/index.html, accessed February 29, 2024
European Central Bank (n. d. c): Documentation for banking groups which have to report data on securities holdings directly to the ECB, retrieved from https://www.ecb.europa.eu/stats/financial_markets_and_interest_rates/securities/reporting/html/index.en.html, accessed April 11, 2024
European Central Bank (n. d. d): Explanatory note on the ECB Regulation on the collection of granular credit and credit risk data, retrieved from https://www.ecb.europa.eu/stats/money_credit_banking/anacredit/html/index.en.html, accessed February 13, 2024
European Central Bank (n. d. e): Making banks' data reporting more efficient, retrieved from https://www.ecb.europa.eu/stats/ecb_statistics/co-operation_and_standards/reporting/html/index.en.html, accessed February 22, 2024
European Central Bank (n. d. f): MFI interest rates, retrieved from https://www.ecb.europa.eu/stats/financial_markets_and_interest_rates/bank_interest_rates/mfi_interest_rates/html/index.en.html, accessed April 15, 2024
European Central Bank (n. d. g): The Banks' Integrated Reporting Dictionary, retrieved from https://bird.ecb.europa.eu/projectDefinition, accessed February 20, 2024
European Central Bank (n. d. h): What makes a bank significant?, retrieved from https://www.bankingsupervision.europa.eu/banking/list/criteria/html/index.en.html, accessed February 6, 2024
European Central Bank (2017): SMCube Information Model, retrieved from https://www.ecb.europa.eu/stats/ecb_statistics/co-operation_and_standards/smcube/shared/files/SMCubeInformationModel201707.pdf, accessed February 21, 2024
European Central Bank (2019): BIRD Technical Guidelines (Release 5.0), retrieved from https://www.ecb.europa.eu/stats/ecb_statistics/co-operation_and_standards/reporting/html/BIRD_Technical_Guidelines_5.0.en.pdf, accessed March 1, 2024
European Central Bank (2020): The ESCB input into the EBA feasibility report under article 430c of the Capital Requirements Regulation (CRR 2), retrieved from https://www.ecb.europa.eu/pub/pdf/other/ecb.escbinputintoebafeasibilityreport092020~eac9cf6102.en.pdf, accessed February 23, 2024
European Central Bank (2022): The Eurosystem Integrated Reporting Framework – an overview, retrieved from https://www.ecb.europa.eu/pub/pdf/other/ecb.escbirefoverview202011~ebb404b7b6.en.pdf, accessed February 20, 2024
European Central Bank (2024a): The Banks' Integrated Reporting Dictionary, retrieved from https://bird.ecb.europa.eu/view/Framework/1544692898335?published=true, accessed March 1, 2024
European Central Bank (2024b): Validation rules in the context of BIRD, retrieved from https://www.ecb.europa.eu/stats/ecb_statistics/co-operation_and_standards/reporting/html/IL_EIL_Validation_rules_latestVersion.pdf, accessed February 29, 2024
European Central Bank / Banco de Espana (2019): Mapping SDMX-XBRL/DPM, retrieved from https://sdmx.org/wp-content/uploads/SDMX-DPM_mapping_version_1_4_7.pdf, accessed February 24, 2024

European Commission (n.d.): Prudential requirements, retrieved from https://finance.ec.europa.eu/banking/banking-regulation/prudential-requirements_en, accessed April 15, 2024

Feraboli, K. / Häkkinen, H. / Gutiérrez, J. (2015): A new indicator for the cost of borrowing in the euro area, 2015, retrieved from https://econpapers.repec.org/bookchap/bisbisifc/39-05.htm, accessed March 19, 2024

Ferran, E. (2016): The Existential Search of the European Banking Authority, in: European Business Organization Law Review, 17/3, pp. 285–317

Freund, E. / Gutsche, L. (2022): A reporting system for the future, Feasibility study on "Redesign Options for Regulatory Reporting", retrieved from https://www.bafin.de/SharedDocs/Downloads/EN/Anlage/dl_anlage_fa_bj_machbarkeitsstudie_meldewesen_en.html;jsessionid=944C38E7CB941B4F94D30ACC5AD6AF7D.internet012?nn=19586540, accessed February 22, 2024

Goodhart, C. / Sato, H. (2024): A note on the differences between European and international methodologies of banking regulation and supervision, London School of Economics and Political Science, LSE Library, 2024, retrieved from https://econpapers.repec.org/paper/ehllserod/122044.htm, accessed April 11, 2024

Gustafsson, J. (2017): Single case studies vs. multiple case studies: A comparative study, Academy of Business, Engineering and Science Halmstad University, retrieved from https://www.diva-portal.org/smash/get/diva2:1064378/fulltext01.pdf, accessed April 19, 2024

Haentjens, M. (2020): European Banking and Financial Law 2e, 2nd ed., Milton: Taylor & Francis Group

Hahn, F. (2010): Financial Market Regulation, in: Austrian Economic Quarterly, 15(1), pp. 94–97

Halpin, T. (2008): Information modeling and relational databases, The Morgan Kaufmann series in data management systems, 2nd ed., Amsterdam/Boston, Mass.: Morgan Kaufman; Safari Books Online

Harnay, S. / Scialom, L. (2016): The influence of the economic approaches to regulation on banking regulations: a short history of banking regulations, in: Cambridge Journal of Economics, 40/2, pp. 401–426

Hille, E. (2013): Recent developments in restructuring the Austrian banking reporting system, in: Journal of Banking Regulation, 14/3-4, pp. 269–284

IBM (n.d.): What is data modeling?, retrieved from https://www.ibm.com/topics/data-modeling, accessed April 10, 2024

Israël, J.-M. (2018): SDD, BIRD, IReF, AnaCredit and RIAD Integrated Reporting, what could we aim at?, retrieved from https://www.bancaditalia.it/pubblicazioni/altri-atti-convegni/2018-cooperazione/2-Jean-Marc_Israel.pdf, accessed February 21, 2024

Kaetzler, J. / Richter, U. (2015): The supervision of financial institutions in the EU, retrieved from https://cms-lawnow.com/en/regzone/articles/2015/07/the-supervision-of-financial-institutions-in-the-eu?format=pdf&v=12, accessed April 10, 2024

Keune, C. (2015): Rechtliche Grundlagen und Grenzen der EIOPA, Düsseldorfer Reihe, v.25, s.l.: Verlag Versicherungswirtschaft GmbH

Kienecker, K. / Sedlacek Günther / Turner, J. (2018): Managing the processing chain from banks' source data to statistical and regulatory reports in Austria, in: OeNB Statistiken, 3, retrieved from http://www.oenb.at/dam/jcr:d9cdbe0a-a6d4-409a-8ac5-670cad2619b0/05_kienecker_statistiken_3_18.pdf, accessed April 3, 2024

Kleres, J. (2015): Emotional expertise: emotions and the expert interview, in: Flam, H. (Hrsg.): Methods of exploring emotions, London/New York: ROUTLEDGE, pp. 110–120

Kloos, S. / Westerberg, C. / Bernreuther Marius (2022): BIRD 6.0 – Weg zum integrierten Reporting-Framework, retrieved from https://bankinghub.de/banksteuerung/bird-6-0#:~:text=Der%20IReF%20Collection%20Layer%20repr%C3%A4sentiert,Initiative%20f%C3%BCr%20Banken%20und%20Aufsicht., accessed March 20, 2024

Lintner, P. / Lincoln Nagy, M. / Pyziak, P. / Godwin, A. / Schroeder, S. / Irsalieva, N. (2017): Understanding bank recovery and resolution in the EU: a guidebook to the BRRD, Washington, D.C.: World Bank Group

Liu, L. / Özsu, M. (eds.) (2009): Encyclopedia of Database Systems, SpringerLink Bücher, Boston, MA: Springer US, retrieved from http://www.springerlink.com/content/978-0-387-35544-3/#section=380154&page=1&locus=0

Lux, J. / Piechocki, M. (2015): Paradigmenwechsel im Meldewesen - der österreichische Ansatz als Modell für Deutschland?, in: Zeitschrift für das gesamte Kreditwesen, 13, pp. 661–663, retrieved from https://www.kreditwesen.de/kreditwesen/themenschwerpunkte/aufsaetze/paradigmenwechsel-meldewesen-oesterreichische-ansatz-modell-id28677.html, accessed February 19, 2024

Masera, R. (2014): CRR/CRD IV: The Trees and the Forest, in: SSRN Electronic Journal, pp. 381–422, retrieved from https://papers.ssrn.com/sol3/papers.cfm?abstract_id=2418215, accessed April 9, 2024

Mayring, P. (2014): Qualitative content analysis: theoretical foundation, basic procedures and software solution, Klagenfurt, retrieved from https://www.ssoar.info/ssoar/handle/document/39517, accessed April 21, 2024

Mohajan, H. (2018): Qualitative research methodology in social sciences and related subjects, in: Journal of Economic Development, Environment and People, 7/1, pp. 23–48, retrieved from https://www.ceeol.com/search/article-detail?id=640546, accessed April 19, 2024

Montalbano, G. (ed.) (2021): Competing interest groups and lobbying in the construction of the European Banking Union. Dissertation [xix, 337 Seiten], LUISS Guido Carli Free International University: Springer International Publishing

Mora, J. (2020): Experiences with DPM in a Supervisor, retrieved from https://2020.eurofiling.info/wp-content/uploads/DPM_3_JavierMora.pdf, accessed April 10, 2024

Mostajabi, F. / Safaei, A. / Sahafi Amir (2021): A Systematic Review of Data Models for the Big Data Problem, in: IEEE Access, 9, pp. 128889–128904

Müller, M. (2020): INVENTIVE FRC – FINANCE: EUROPÄISCHE DATENHARMONISIERUNG IM RAHMEN VON BIRD UND IREF ALS CHANCE ZUR KOSTENSENKUNG, retrieved from https://www.capgemini.com/de-de/insights/blog/inventive-frc-finance-europaeische-datenharmonisierung-bird-iref/, accessed March 27, 2024

Novak, P. / Muchna, J. (2023): Banking Risk and Finance Management on Quality Data, retrieved from https://www.pwc.com/cz/en/assets/Bank_Risk_and_Finance_on_Quality_Data-after_design.pdf, accessed April 15, 2024

Oesterreichische Nationalbank (n. d. a): Ableitung der Nominale von Immobiliensicherheiten, retrieved from https://www.oenb.at/mdi/entity/m0b0c4625-e299-48af-b226-fcb701946e83?lang=DE&initWithVersion=5.5, accessed March 25, 2024

Oesterreichische Nationalbank (n. d. b): Beispiele zur Granularen Kredit-Erhebung (GKE), retrieved from https://www.oenb.at/mdi/entity/m534fdfd4-f910-4478-8aaf-a6c4500a923a?lang=DE&initWithVersion=5.6, accessed April 2, 2024

Oesterreichische Nationalbank (n. d. c): Integrated Reporting Data Model, retrieved from https://www.myoenb.com/opus/login, accessed April 11, 2024

Oesterreichische Nationalbank (n. d. d): Integrated Reporting Data Model, retrieved from https://www.oenb.at/en/reporting/integrated-reporting-data-model.html, accessed February 19, 2024

Oesterreichische Nationalbank (n. d. e): Meldewesen, retrieved from https://www.oenb.at/meldewesen.html, accessed February 25, 2024

Oesterreichische Nationalbank (n. d. f): Single Supervisory Mechanism, retrieved from https://www.oenb.at/en/financial-market/three-pillars-banking-union/single-supervisory-mechanism.html, accessed April 10, 2024

Oesterreichische Nationalbank (n. d. g): The three pillars of the banking union, retrieved from https://www.oenb.at/en/financial-market/three-pillars-banking-union.html, accessed February 6, 2024

Oesterreichische Nationalbank (n. d. h): The three pillars of the banking union, retrieved from https://www.oenb.at/en/financial-market/three-pillars-banking-union.html, accessed April 10, 2024

Pinder, J. (2018): The European Union. A very short introduction, Oxford: Oxford University Press

Pinheiro, C. (2014): EUROPEAN UNION BALANCE OF PAYMENTS AND INTERNATIONAL, retrieved from https://policycommons.net/artifacts/2182467/european-union-balance-of-payments-and-international/2938444/, accessed April 9, 2024

Plumlee, D. / Plumlee, M. (2008): Assurance on XBRL for Financial Reporting, retrieved from https://papers.ssrn.com/sol3/papers.cfm?abstract_id=1104245, accessed February 16, 2024

Richards, J. / Smith, B. / Saeedi, A. (2006): An Introduction to XBRL, in: SSRN Electronic Journal, retrieved from https://papers.ssrn.com/sol3/papers.cfm?abstract_id=1007570, accessed April 9, 2024

Romano, S. / Martinez-Heras, J. / Natalini Raponi, F. / Guidi, G. / Gottron, T. (2021): Discovering new plausibility checks for supervisory data: a machine learning approach, retrieved from https://www.ecb.europa.eu/pub/pdf/scpsps/ecb.sps41~b3f9939b22.en.pdf, accessed April 9, 2024

Rossi, C. / Gillet, S. (2020): EBA DPM 3.0, INSIGHTS AND IMPACTS, retrieved from https://www.reply.com/avantage-reply/en/Shared%20Documents/Regulatory-Reporting%E2%80%93Impacts-and-Insights-for-The-Data-Point-Model-3.0.pdf, accessed February 19, 2024

Salou, G. (2008): The ECB Statistical Data Warehouse: improving data accessibility for all users, retrieved from https://www.biz.org/ifc/publ/ifcb28.pdf#page=319, accessed April 9, 2024

Sanction Scanner (n.d.): European Banking System, retrieved from https://sanctionscanner.com/blog/european-banking-system-427, accessed April 15, 2024

SAP (2023): Understanding Relationship Types in SAP CAP: One-to-One, One-to-Many, and Many-to-Many, retrieved from https://community.sap.com/t5/technology-blogs-by-sap/understanding-relationship-types-in-sap-cap-one-to-one-one-to-many-and-many/ba-p/13567606, accessed April 15, 2024

Schammo, P. (2011): The European Securities and Markets Authority: Lifting the veil on the allocation of powers, in: Common Market Law Review, 48/Issue 6, pp. 1879–1913

Scheller, H. (2006): The European Central Bank. History, role and functions, Eurosystem, 2nd ed., Frankfurt am Main: Europ. Central Bank

Shavshukov, V. / Zhuravleva, N. (2023): National and International Financial Market Regulation and Supervision Systems: Challenges and Solutions, in: Journal of Risk and Financial Management, 16/6, p. 289, retrieved from https://www.mdpi.com/1911-8074/16/6/289, accessed April 9, 2024

Singerová, J. (2015): XBRL: Different Approach of Utilization, in: 2212–5671, 25, pp. 134–140, retrieved from https://www.sciencedirect.com/science/article/pii/s2212567115007212, accessed April 9, 2024

Single Resolution Board (2024): 2024 Resolution Reporting, retrieved from https://www.srb.europa.eu/en/content/2024-resolution-reporting, accessed February 20, 2024

StatSilk (2021): SDMX Introduction with Simple SDMX-ML Example and Tutorial, retrieved from https://www.statsilk.com/sdmx/sdmx-introduction-simple-sdmx-ml-example-and-tutorial, accessed April 9, 2024

Stindt, G. / Schönfelder, B. (2014): Finanzinformationen gemäß FINREP–die Einführung harmonisierter Meldeanforderungen, in: Zeitschrift für das gesamte Kreditwesen, 13, pp. 652–656, retrieved from https://www.kreditwesen.de/mimas/system/files/content/articledownloads/2015/09/zf_14_13_652-656.pdf, accessed April 3, 2024

Sutterer, T. (2021): Supervisory Reporting: DPM, ITS & Validierungsregeln kurz erklärt, retrieved from https://www.movisco.de/blog/supervisory-reporting-dpm-its-validierungsregeln, accessed February 16, 2024

Teixeira, P. (2017): The Legal History of the Banking Union, in: European Business Organization Law Review, 18/3, pp. 535–565

Turner, J. / Sedlacek, G. (2015): European Reporting Framework–a possible solution to reporting challenges for banks, retrieved from https://2015.isiproceedings.org/files/sts010-p2-s.pdf, accessed April 8, 2024

Wildemuth, B. / Zhang, Y. (2017): Applications of social research methods to questions in information and library science, Santa Barbara, California/Denver, Colorado: Libraries Unlimited

Wolle, B. (2014): Risikomanagementsysteme in Versicherungsunternehmen. Von regulatorischen Vorgaben zum nachhaltigen Risikomanagement, IT im Unternehmen, Wiesbaden: Springer Vieweg

WU Wien (n.d.): Cardinalities, retrieved from https://www.wu.ac.at/erp/webtrainer/erm-webtrainer/theory, accessed April 10, 2024

XBRL (2021): xBRL-CSV and Granular Data: the AnaCredit example, a Proof of Concept from XBRL Europ, retrieved from https://www.xbrl.org/xbrl-csv-and-granular-data-the-anacredit-example-a-proof-of-concept-from-xbrl-europe/, accessed April 10, 2024